Jobs, Dollars, and EEO:

How to Hire More Productive Entry-Level Workers

RICHARD A. FEAR

JAMES F. ROSS

McGraw-Hill Book Company

New York   St. Louis   San Francisco   Auckland   Bogotá
Hamburg   Johannesburg   London   Madrid   Mexico
Montreal   New Delhi   Panama   Paris   São Paulo
Singapore   Sydney   Tokyo   Toronto

Library of Congress Cataloging in Publication Data

Fear, Richard A.
   Jobs, dollars, and EEO.

   Includes index.
   1. Employee selection—United States.
2. Affirmative action programs—United States.
I. Ross, James F.   II. Title.   III. Title: Jobs,
dollars, and E.E.O.
HF5549.5.S38F4   658.3'112   82-274
ISBN 0-07-020199-4   AACR2

1 2 3 4 5 6 7 8 9 0   DODO   8 9 8 7 6 5 4 3 2

ISBN 0-07-020199-4

*The editors for this book were William R. Newton and William B. O'Neal,
the designer was Richard A. Roth, and the production supervisor was Thomas
G. Kowalczyk. It was set in Caledonia by Datapage.*

Printed and bound by R. R. Donnelley & Sons Company

ABOUT THE AUTHORS

A registered psychologist, **Richard A. Fear** graduated from Middlebury College and did his graduate study at Boston University and the University of Southern California. He has lectured in applied psychology at the School of Business, Columbia University, and more recently has lectured at The Johns Hopkins University.

He spent 27 years with The Psychological Corporation of New York City, where he eventually served as vice president in charge of the Industrial Division. In 1969 he established his own consulting firm, Interviewer Training Services, and since that time has devoted all his energy to interviewer training. Over the years, he has trained several thousand corporate managers and personnel people in this country and abroad in the techniques of the interview.

He coauthored his first book, *Employee Evaluation Manual for Interviewers*, in 1943, a book which remained in print for 30 years. He wrote *The Evaluation Interview*, a McGraw-Hill publication, in 1958 and published subsequent editions and revisions in 1973 and 1978. In its second edition, *The Evaluation Interview* won the American Society for Personnel Administration award as the "most outstanding human resource management book published in 1973." This book has been in continuous publication for 24 years and has grossed a million dollars.

James F. Ross graduated from Washington and Jefferson College with a degree in psychology and has done graduate study at Purdue University.

He began his career with Bethlehem Steel in 1969 as a member of that corporation's management training program. His initial assignment, to one of Bethlehem's major steelmaking facilities, involved the design and validation of preemployment tests and the development and implementation of a nationwide recruitment program. That program provided thousands of hourly and salaried personnel for entry-level, craft, and supervisory positions that opened up because of a major plant expansion. During that time he was also responsible for developing administrative procedures and an organizational structure for the personnel department.

In 1973 he was promoted and transferred to Bethlehem's corporate industrial relations staff. There he assumed responsibility for coordinating the implementation of that corporation's equal employment opportunity (EEO) programs at its steel plants, mining operations, shipyards, and subsidiary companies. In this assignment he directs the activities of internal EEO and personnel reviews, institutes corrective measures, and represents Bethlehem at government compliance reviews.

In addition to his EEO responsibilities, his present assignment involves the design and implementation of cost-effective selection procedures for Bethlehem operations and the direction of the corporation's out-placement programs.

CONTENTS

CHAPTER ELEVEN. Interpretation—An Overview . . .   148

CHAPTER TWELVE. Interpreting Work History   161

PREFACE

To our knowledge, no writer in recent years has addressed, exclusively, the selection of entry-level production, maintenance, office, or clerical workers, nor has anyone taken the trouble to investigate the cost of hiring a single entry-level employee. Yet our findings indicate that the cost of hiring and maintaining a poorly qualified worker over a probation period that may last as long as 3 months ranges between $5000 and $7000. In view of the fact that many companies lose 40 percent or more of the persons hired in a given year, the cost is staggering, and this is a cost of which most managers are completely unaware.

Turnover, absenteeism, and poor quality of work have increased alarmingly during the past decade because many companies have resorted to indiscriminate hiring, based on the false assumption that equal employment opportunity (EEO) regulations permit nothing more. However, we have made a careful study of EEO regulations, and this, together with our firsthand encounters with government compliance officers and investigators, has convinced us that much more can be done within these regulations than most people realize.

This book is concerned first of all with an overview of EEO regulations in terms of what can and what cannot be done. The main thrust here is a series of proven techniques that will substantially reduce any company's vulnerability to government intervention. One unanticipated result of our investigations was the discovery that the attainment of affirmative action goals can actually strengthen a personnel department and increase its effectiveness. Internal auditing procedures, in particular, have been found not only to reduce substantially charges of discrimination but also to eliminate unnecessary paperwork.

A newly developed selection program for entry-level workers, however, represents the most important aspect of this book. This program has been in operation in a major corporation at several of its divisions over a period of 2 years and has been found to reduce turnover, absenteeism, tardiness, grievances, accidents, and compensation cases substantially, at the same time satisfying all EEO requirements. We have discussed this program in considerable detail, from the newly developed application form to the preliminary interview, the aptitude tests, the medical examination, and finally the employment interview itself. We have also outlined procedures for developing worker specifications and making reference checks. Finally, the book contains an interview guide specifically designed for the selection of hourly employees.

Those who are familiar with *The Evaluation Interview* by Richard Fear will note that some of the methodology in that book finds its way into the discussion of the employment interview in this book. We have drawn upon that source because the methodology is just as timely today as it was 24 years ago and remains in use in many personnel departments today.

We hope that this book, in some small way, will help to reverse the trend toward indiscriminate hiring. We have tried to show that sound personnel practices can still be utilized and that good selection standards can still be maintained.

In the development of techniques discussed in this book, we have drawn upon our many years of personnel and consulting experience as a principal source, but we are indebted to colleagues, past and present, who have contributed valuable ideas along the way.

RICHARD A. FEAR
JAMES F. ROSS

PART ONE

Equal Employment Opportunity

CHAPTER ONE

The Cost of Poor Selection and EEO Litigation

The selection of entry-level plant and office personnel has been largely neglected in the current literature. Most books on this subject have been concerned with the selection of professional or managerial employees. In sharp contrast, this book deals exclusively with the selection of entry-level hourly and clerical personnel, with emphasis on innovative methods of selecting the best-qualified individuals within the framework of equal employment opportunity (EEO) regulations.

This book provides a practical, hands-on approach designed for use by small companies employing fewer than 50 people as well as by large corporations that may employ many thousands. It is useful, moreover, for the selection of both blue-collar and clerical workers.

THE COST FACTOR

Operating managers have finally faced up to the fact that mistakes in the selection of candidates for key positions cost their companies a great deal of money. But few such managers are aware of the staggering costs that result from the selection of poorly qualified people at the entry level. Although a single mistake in the selection of a person for a key job obviously amounts to a great deal more than a mistake in the selection of an hourly worker, the total cost of poor selection at the entry level is far greater, in light of the larger number of people involved.

An analysis of cost factors involved in selecting poorly qualified employees who either fail or are marginal producers involves the examination of *tangible costs* and *intangible costs*. Tangible costs include:

1. The administrative costs involved in recruiting, interviewing, administering physical examinations, and enrolling the employee in payroll and benefit programs
2. The costs of the employee's salary
3. The costs of the employee's benefit programs
4. The cost of training the employee (both formally and on the job)

Intangible costs involve:

1. Possible loss in production
2. Loss of potential improvement in productivity that could have been realized by hiring more productive workers
3. Increased costs resulting from employee attendance problems, accidents, union contract grievances, worker compensation costs, incidents of employee discipline problems, and social insurance program costs

In a typical analysis utilizing tangible cost factors, selection of a $12,000-a-year plant or office employee who failed after 3 months would result in the following loss:

Salary (Few entry-level jobs pay less than $12,000 a year.)	**$3000**
Benefits (Usually considered 30 percent of salary.)	900
Training (Most new employees get 40 hours of formal or on-the-job training during the first 3 months.)	500 min.
Administration (Recruitment, employment, and medical services.)	600 min.
Other costs due to absenteeism, tardiness, illness, accidents, etc. (Not listed because situations vary widely.)	
Total	$5000

It could, of course, be argued that the $3000 salary listed above is not a complete loss because the new employee does some useful work during the 3-month period. As a poorly qualified new employee, however, the individual's productive usefulness will be largely negated by such intangible factors as the increased amount of the supervisor's time required, possible accidents, possible damage to equipment, and contribution to poor morale in the immediate work force.

It could be further argued that the $900 listed above for benefits should not be included for a person who stays with the company only for 3 months or less. The fact of the matter is, though, that most employers contribute to benefit funds for every hour that *each* employee works. Short-term employees also have an effect on employers' state unemployment tax costs.

The tangible costs mentioned above obviously represent a bare minimum since entry-level jobs in many industries may pay as much as $18,000 per year and since training costs in some industries involve as many as 40 hours of training in safety alone. However, even a $5000 minimum cost of selecting the wrong person, when multiplied by the number of people who are lost in a given year through poor selection, can amount to hundreds of thousands of dollars—an enormous bite out of company profits.

The cost of developing better selection procedures and of training employment interviewers—the core of this book—is small indeed considering the potential savings involved. When one considers that many companies suffer as much as 40 percent turnover in a given year, even a small improvement of 20 or 30 percent in the selection batting average would more than pay for the complete operation of an efficient, cost-effective employment office.

The manager of a large construction operation was recently shocked when confronted with an analysis of cost factors resulting from poor selection of unskilled workers. At that facility, where the average hourly wage for unskilled workers is $10.50 an hour exclusive of benefits and where the employee probationary period is 240 hours, application of the analysis demonstrated above resulted in an estimate of a tangible loss of $6800 for each individual who failed during the probationary period. At this facility 85 persons were terminated because of their inability to perform during the probationary period. The 85 persons discharged, multiplied by the $6800 cost per individual separated, amounted to a total figure of $578,000. Since this figure represented a direct loss over a period of only 6 weeks, the total loss for the year would obviously be enormous. Interesting enough, however, few managers are aware of the tremendous costs incurred by the employment of inefficient and poorly qualified workers. Once confronted with the facts, though, they become highly motivated to do something about this situation.

The design and implementation of cost-effective selection systems not only can save a great deal of money by reducing turnover but also can have a major impact in reducing all other employment costs, as we shall see later. As might be expected, productivity improves as well.

Charges of Discrimination— An Immense Financial Burden

At any given time, most large corporations will have *several hundred* separate charges of discrimination, ranging from methods used in recruiting all the way to discharge policies. Smaller organizations will, of course, have their proportionate number of such charges. Although some charges of discrimination may have resulted from conscious unwillingness to consider minorities, women, and the handicapped for certain jobs, the vast majority stem from carelessness and ignorance of the law. Let it be said, too, that many discrimination charges have no basis in any kind of fact.

The total cost of processing cases of discrimination is obviously tremendous. Case preparation and the time required of important people for case conferences and court appearances average 40 expensive hours per case. When outside legal assistance is required, another $10,000 to $20,000 per case must be added. This places an enormous burden on American industry. It can, of course, be argued that industry has brought this burden on itself through past inequitable practices; however, be that as it may, the burden of discrimination charges has had a remarkable and predictable effect on American industry.

Personnel managers in many companies have panicked in the sense that they have taken the position that true selection of entry-level employees is no longer possible. Because of the fear of running afoul of EEO regulations, they have given up all employment tests, downgraded their interviewers to "paper processors," and in many cases reverted to indiscriminate selection or hiring at random.

The authors take the view, however, that it is still quite possible —within the legal confines of EEO regulations—to select the best-qualified persons available. In the chapters that follow, we will show that companies *can* give aptitude and dexterity tests, that they *can* train interviewers to select the best-qualified people from among those available, and that they *can*, in fact, *reject* those minority and women applicants who do not measure up to the requirements of the job. If this were not true, some companies might not be able to remain in business, particularly since they now have to compete with industry in countries such as Japan and West Germany. Certainly, the sponsors of EEO did not have this in mind. On March 4, 1981, the Supreme Court confirmed this view in a decision rejecting the employment discrimination test being used by the Eighth U.S. Circuit Court of Appeals in St. Louis. In his opinion reflecting the unanimous decision of the Court, Justice Lewis F. Powell, Jr., said that the law "does not demand that an employer give preferential treatment to minorities or women. The employer has discretion to choose among equally qualified candidates."

Loss of Productivity

It is now widely understood that decreasing productivity is a major cause of inflation. As the labor costs of producing the end product increase, so must the price of that product. Obviously, inefficient and poorly motivated workers—many of whom have been selected at random—contribute significantly to higher labor costs. We do not mean to imply, however, that better selection of employees represents the only way to increase productivity. Many companies in this country are in great need of plant modernization, particularly with respect to the increased use of automation.

We are told, for example, that the wider use of robots is inevitable. Robots can be programmed to accomplish many jobs which human beings find dangerous, distasteful, or so routinized that boredom is inescapable. Moreover, robots do not get sick, do not need rest breaks, do not pile up pension benefits, and can function with far greater accuracy than a human being can.

Japan has been the first country in the world to recognize and make widespread use of the contribution that robots can make. A report in the December 8, 1980, issue of *Time* magazine revealed that Japan has some 10,000 robots operating in its industrial complex today, while the United States is second with only 3000. It is logical to assume that this represents one important reason why Japan poses such a serious threat to Detroit—why that country can export its automobiles over vast distances and still compete effectively in terms of both economics and quality.

Some economists maintain that the use of robots will become so widespread that a second industrial revolution may be in the making. If this should develop, many workers will lose their present jobs and will have to be retrained for other positions. And who will be the most likely workers to be replaced by machines? The poorly educated, unskilled high school dropouts. These are the people who make up a large segment of assembly line production—the type of job for which robots can be most easily programmed.

Unemployment among the unskilled and poorly educated is already a most serious problem in this country. If such unemployment is permitted to increase appreciably, social upheaval of huge proportions could very easily ensue. The recent riots in England are an example. This is why all branches of government, the public educational system, and all segments of industry must work together to develop an extensive retraining program for unskilled workers. Industry's possible role in this undertaking will be treated in a subsequent chapter. Suffice it to say here, however, that prevention is always more effective than treatment of a situation that has been permitted to deteriorate. This means that the public schools must develop much more meaningful, relevant, and imaginative vocational education programs—programs that could do so much to reverse the widespread tendency to drop out of school at 16.

Impact of Mechanization
on Employee Selection

But what does all this have to do with the better selection of entry-level people? Well, for one thing, we shall undoubtedly have a larger pool of unskilled people from which to choose the best-qualified workers for those entry-level jobs not appropriate for robotization. Given the proper tools, interviewers should become more effective as the number of individuals from which a single worker can be selected increases. Thus, if it becomes possible to choose one in ten instead of one in two or three, it is only reasonable to assume that better selection should take place.

We have seen from examples cited earlier in this chapter how enormously costly poor selection at the entry level can be. If we can substantitally reduce the number of workers who fail to make it or who leave of their own accord, we shall, of course, have a more stable work force. This means less likelihood of interruption of production schedules. It also means that supervisors can spend more of their time getting the product "out the door," rather than breaking in new workers.

With the robotization of many current entry-level positions, such as routine assembly jobs, the entry level for jobs will be higher and will more often require *skills* of one type or another. If industry can find applicants who have already been trained in these skills, on-the-job training will be reduced appreciably, thus permitting the concentration of more time and energy on getting the job done. This again highlights the tremendous contribution that could be made by a revitalized vocational education program in the public schools, as well as by more relevant retraining programs sponsored by the state and federal governments. Industry's role in this retraining program can very well take the form of affirmative action, as we shall see later.

INTERVIEWERS IN A CRITICAL ROLE

In those companies where interviewers have not been reduced to paper processors, the interviewer's job has become more complex and more critical than ever before. On the one hand, interviewers are expected to assist management in improving productivity and reducing turnover by selecting the best possible candidate for blue-collar as well as clerical positions. On the other hand, they are expected to do this in such a way as not to invite charges of discrimination; a tall task indeed in light of the complexity of EEO regulations. Within the EEO guidelines, interviewers are expected to select a sufficient number of qualified people to meet peak periods of demand without increasing the number of employees involved in the selection decision. Moreover, today's interviewers wear many hats; in addition to hiring they are also involved in postinterview counseling, explanation of benefit programs, exit interviews, and even the task of convincing some applicants to accept jobs with their companies.

Interviewers have, of course, been told that they cannot employ any method that would be considered discriminatory or that would be in violation of federal, state, or local regulations affecting EEO. However, they have been told this in such a way that many now believe they have been stripped of the basic tools formerly used in the selection process. Management has become so alarmed by the millions of dollars lost every year in processing cases of discrimination that some top executives now tend to bend over backward in their efforts to reduce such losses. In so doing, many have unnecessarily relinquished important management prerogatives—prerogatives that they vitally need in order to stay in business. It is probably not an exaggeration to say that most interviewers today are foundering in a sea of uncertainty. They are charged with the responsibility of doing an effective selection job but have been told that many of the techniques they would like to use are now illegal.

The interviewers' major problem stems from the fact that they are attempting to select candidates without the guidance and assistance of a cost-effective selection system. Some interviewers have even been led to believe, for example, that it is no longer possible to confirm an applicant's prior work record by asking a former employer to verify dates of employment and type of job held, as one means of determining job stability. Nothing could be further from the truth.

Training of Interviewers
an Absolute Necessity

It has long been acknowledged by impartial observers that interviewers receive less formal training in how to carry out their responsibilities than do any other important people in industry. Accounting people get long years of training, labor-relations people get very careful and lengthy indoctrination, people handling employee benefits are carefully schooled, and even typists and stenographers come to industry with substantial preparation. But what kind of training do most interviewers get? Very little indeed. They are expected to learn by doing, by trial and error. As bad as this has always been, it has become almost *dangerous* in today's world. Ignorance of important provisions of the law, alone, can get interviewers into the kind of trouble that could conceivably cost their companies a great amount of money.

Some companies—those with more farsighted and sophisticated management—have at long last embarked upon training programs designed to improve selection. When improved selection systems have been developed, those companies bring their interviewers together for several days of orientation and training. These sessions are devoted to a careful scrutiny of the law, with emphasis on what it is still possible to do within EEO guidelines and on those things that must be avoided. These companies are inaugurating training programs they should have undertaken years ago. They are turning to consultants for assistance in developing selection systems and in the training of interviewers in modern methods of evaluating people.

SELECTION PROCEDURES HAVE BEEN PROVED COST-EFFECTIVE

Systems, methods, and procedures described in this book are based upon many years of practical experience and, as such, are factual rather than theoretical. As a matter of interest, these selection procedures are already in place at a number of facilities and, in one such facility, have been evaluated and found to be cost-effective. As a result of a validation study conducted at this facility, the selection procedures were shown to have enabled the company to hire better-qualified applicants, ensured the attainment of all affirmative action goals, met the requirements of federal regulations on employee selection procedures, and actually reduced employment-office costs.

In order to ensure that the validation study undertaken by this company met the provisions of federal regulations on employee selection procedures and was technically sound, the expertise of a respected outside consultant was obtained. That individual approved the design of the study.

The study was carried out in a large manufacturing plant with two sample groups and involved more than 900 employees. Each group was tracked for the first 24 months of employment. Group A, the control group, consisted of employees who had been hired *before* the new selection procedures were installed, and group B involved employees who had been hired *after* the new selection program was inaugurated. Unlike most studies that utilize *subjective* criteria such as supervisor ratings, this study drew upon *objective* criteria such as turnover, absenteeism, tardiness, grievances filed, accidents, social insurance program (SIP) claims, compensation cases, and recorded disciplinary actions. The data were further analyzed with respect to race and sex. The major findings of this study are discussed below in terms of the variables indicated.

Savings

The new selection procedures reduced the turnover rate by a remarkable 28 percent. The decrease in administrative and training costs alone amounted to over $300,000 per year. Since the selection procedures in use prior to the introduction of the new methodology were considered to be quite good, the results are all the more significant. Had the study been conducted in a company where the new procedures were compared with indiscriminate hiring, the reduction in turnover could quite obviously have been substantially higher. The authors are familiar with two such studies conducted in other companies where the reduction of turnover approached 40 percent. When intangible savings involving such factors as productivity and better utilization of super-

TABLE 1   Effect of Improved Selection Procedures on Employee Problems

	Group A (1977–1978)		Group B (1979–1980)		
	No. of occurrences*	Average per employee	No. of occurrences†	Average per employee	Average reduction, %
Days absent	14,043	25.80	5,486	15.07	−42
Days late	3,575	6.57	1,527	4.20	−36
Grievances filed	121	0.22	13	0.04	−82
Accidents reported	843	1.55	426	1.17	−25
SIP claims	458	0.84	149	0.41	−51
Compensation cases	63	0.12	29	0.08	−33
Disciplinary actions	3,254	5.98	1,352	3.71	−38

* $N = 370$ whites (68.1%) + 174 minority employees (31.9%) = 544 total.
† $N = 258$ whites (70.9%) + 106 minority employees (29.1%) = 364 total.

TABLE 2   Reductions (by Race and Sex) in Employee Problems Due to Improved Selection Procedures

	Total, %	White male, %	Minority male, %	Female, %
Absenteeism	42	42	30	46
Tardiness	36	50	23	40
Grievances	82	84	80	88
Accidents	25	50	100+	50
Insurance claims	51	68	53	46
Compensation cases	33	36	13	25
Disciplinary action	38	40	28	64

visors' time are considered, the overall results of reduced turnover assume critical importance.

Additional results of this study, concerned with absenteeism, tardiness, grievances, accidents, SIP claims, worker compensation cases, and disciplinary actions, are shown in Table 1. Table 2 provides a further analysis of average reductions, by race and sex, following improved selection procedures.

It will be noted from Tables 1 and 2 that there was a substantial reduction in all categories between control group A and group B and that the reduction for females was greater than that for minority males. When these reductions were converted into dollars, employment costs were found to have been reduced by in excess of $1 million. It will be noted that the items considered do not include salary and benefits, consideration of which would add to the savings. The total savings of over $1 million equates to approximately $3000 per employee hired.

The largest segment of the total savings resulted from reduction of absenteeism—$569,268. The reduction in days absent amounted to a reduction of 18 employees (adjusted for the difference in the size of the two groups) who did not have to be hired because of improved attendance. The 1980 hourly wage cost, including fringe benefits, was $31,626, and this multiplied by 18 provides the figure noted above.

The turnover rate among the 1977 and 1979 groups was reduced by 28 percent. Of the 544 persons hired in 1977, 150 were terminated, but, of the 364 persons hired in 1979, only 72 were terminated, an actual reduction of 78 employees terminated. The actual dollar reduction was 78 times the $4514 for administrative and training costs, or $352,092.

The third-largest saving, $131,880, resulted from reduction of 157 SIP claims, again adjusted for the difference in the size of the two groups. In order to place a reliable dollar figure on the reduction of these claims, 1978 was used as a base year when the average cost was $840 per claim.

Smaller dollar figures resulted from reduction of accidents and compensation cases, but it was not possible to apply dollar figures to days late, grievances filed, or disciplinary cases.

In the company considered in this study, informal results also became readily apparent. Supervisors reported that they were getting much better people, employees seemed to be much more interested in their jobs, and the quality of work improved. Statistical validations permitted the company to continue the use of these procedures in accordance with government regulations and demonstrated that they were free of discriminatory intent.

ASSUME A POSITIVE ATTITUDE

The aforementioned study demonstrates that, in spite of the many real problems involved in the selection of the best possible candidate while meeting obligations required by EEO regulations, much *can* be done. There are creative methods—completely legal —that can be carried out within the confines of government regulations. Careful scrutiny of EEO regulations reveals that industry's hands are not quite as bound as many people believe. Because of current levels of unemployment, moreover, most companies can be more selective since there are more job applicants than job vacancies. Finally, the various state employment agencies stand ready to provide prescreening and referral services.

In order to determine what can be done, we must first direct our attention to the regulations themselves. The chapter that follows, therefore, is devoted entirely to an overview of these regulations, with particular emphasis on what *can* and what *cannot* be done.

CHAPTER TWO

EEO—An Overview

FEDERAL LAWS AND REGULATIONS

The many and varied regulations affecting EEO, whether they are federal, state, or local, can be reduced to two basic precepts:

1. An employer must not discriminate in any manner against an individual on the basis of that individual's race, sex, age, religion, national origin, handicap, or veteran status.

2. Whenever an employer has fewer minority or female employees in its work force than are available in the area work force, that employer must take affirmative action to recruit, hire, and promote such minorities and females.

Before taking an in-depth look at these two concepts, it may be helpful to review briefly the major federal laws and executive orders concerning EEO.

1. Title VII of the Civil Rights Act of 1964
2. The Equal Pay Act of 1963
3. The Age Discrimination in Employment Act of 1967

15

4. Executive Order 11246
5. The Rehabilitation Act of 1973
6. Vietnam-Era Veterans' Readjustment Assistance Act of 1974

Title VII of the Civil Rights Act of 1964

Title VII of the Civil Rights Act bans all forms of discrimination in employment based on consideration of a person's race, color, religion, sex, or national origin. It covers all terms and conditions of employment and holds a company and its supervisors responsible for any discriminatory acts which occur in the workplace. Title VII is administered and enforced by the federal Equal Employment Opportunity Commission (EEOC).

The Equal Pay Act of 1963

The Equal Pay Act prohibits pay differences between male and female workers who are performing equal or substantially equal work, the performance of which requires equal skill, effort, and responsibility and which is performed under similar working conditions. The Equal Pay Act is enforced by the EEOC.

The Age Discrimination in Employment Act of 1967

The Age Discrimination in Employment Act bans discrimination because of age against anyone at least 40 years old but less than 70. Certain state laws prohibit age discrimination against any adult *regardless* of the person's age. Simply put, it is illegal to base any personnel decision on age or otherwise adversely affect a person's status as an employee because of the person's age. This law is enforced by the EEOC.

Executive Order 11246

Executive Order 11246, issued by President Johnson in 1967, applies to all employers with government contracts or subcontracts. The executive order and its implementing regulations prohibit a contractor from discriminating on the basis of race, color, religion, sex, or national origin, but also obliges each contractor to take affirmative action in hiring and advancing in employment qualified minority and female personnel. The contractor's commitment to affirmative action must be set forth in a written affirmative action compliance program at each of its facilities. These programs include goals for hiring and upgrading minorities and women and must be revised annually. Enforcement of Executive Order 11246 is carried out by the Office of Federal Contract Compliance Programs (OFCCP), U.S. Department of Labor.

The Rehabilitation Act of 1973

The Rehabilitation Act requires federal contractors to take affirmative action to hire and promote qualified handicapped persons. A contractor must have a written affirmative action program at each of its facilities which is designed to ensure that qualified handicapped persons are employed, upgraded, and provided reasonable accommodation to facilitate their employability. The OFCCP enforces this law.

The Vietnam-Era Veterans' Readjustment Assistance Act of 1974

The Readjustment Assistance Act very closely parallels the Rehabilitation Act in that it requires affirmative action by federal contractors in hiring and upgrading Vietnam-era veterans and disabled veterans.

What Does All of This Mean?

The foregoing descriptions are not intended to be totally comprehensive. They are reviewed here simply to indicate the key role all personnel representatives have in implementing a policy of nondiscrimination and affirmative action.

These EEO laws and regulations have come into being because society as a whole has not provided equal opportunity and because there persists a great backlog of employment inequity in our country. Eliminating this backlog and preventing its repetition is the responsibility of all members of our society.

While the laws may be numerous and appear complex, compliance with them is substantially assured if interviewers treat each applicant for employment and each employee as they, themselves, would want to be treated. Put another way, no interviewer would want to be rejected for employment or promotion on the basis of his or her race, color of skin, ethnic heritage, religious affiliation, sex, age, or veteran status or on the basis of a handicap unrelated to his or her ability to perform. We are sure that interviewers will agree that these considerations have no relevance in making an employment decision.

Now that we have briefly reviewed the major federal laws and executive orders concerning EEO, let us take a closer look at the concepts of discrimination and affirmative action.

DISCRIMINATION

Although, as indicated later on in this chapter, some voices in this country are being raised against certain aspects of affirmative action, there is rather general agreement that nondiscrimination should be an important aspect of the American way of life. As applied to employee selection, this objective is reaffirmed by the law, which in essence states that employers cannot by action or inaction, overtly or covertly, discriminate against an applicant or employee on the basis of race, sex, national origin, religion, age, handicap, or veteran status.

The word "nondiscrimination" is virtually self-defining. It simply means that a person must not be treated adversely because that person happens to be black, Hispanic, Asian, American Indian, or female. Put another way, it simply means that everyone must be treated *equally*. This is not always easy to accomplish, however, even when one has a genuine desire to do so.

Built-In Prejudice

We are all, of course, the sum total of our inherited factors plus all the influences that have been brought to bear upon us since birth. The kind of person we are today depends, in part at least, upon the early training we received in the home. Thus, if our parents had certain prejudices, such prejudices may very well have rubbed off on us, quite probably without our knowledge or awareness. Hence, whether we realize it or not, most of us have certain built-in prejudices. Regulations dealing with nondiscrimination such as the Civil Rights Act of 1964, therefore, have had the positive effect of forcing us to reexamine our attitudes toward those people who may be somewhat different with respect to appearance, color of skin, methods of communicating, and sociological mores. If interviewers permit their prejudices to preclude the hiring of deserving minorities, women, or handicapped persons, in all likelihood they will ultimately cost their companies hundreds of thousands of dollars in charges of employee discrimination. As a consequence, most employment people are taking a second look at their attitudes toward people and, one hopes, making the necessary corrections.

Some employers fail to hire a minority member or a woman because, in their minds, neither is "suitable" for the work or because "better" candidates are available. As far as their awareness of their own thoughts is concerned, these employers actually believe that they are hiring on merit. What they do not perceive is how their attitudes affect their thinking and behavior.

Discrimination versus Nondiscrimination

The terms "discrimination" and "nondiscrimination" are very commonly used in today's society but also are very much misunderstood. Discrimination is a common, accepted practice. Each of us, in our daily lives, discriminates in our choice of clothing, food, and what we do with our leisure time and with many other aspects of our lives. To discriminate, then, really means to have a choice or preference. To make a choice or to have a preference is normal and accepted. It is unconscionable, however, and, in fact, illegal when that choice or preference is used against people because of race, sex, age, national origin, or physical or mental handicaps.

In their attempts to avoid all aspects of discrimination, interviewers must be eternally vigilant. There are times, for example, when an interviewer conducts a properly job-related interview but, at the completion of the interview, falls into the trap of discussing personal feelings or concerns about a female job applicant seeking employment in a traditional male position or about a minority applicant seeking employment in a job that the interviewer views as a traditional nonminority position. Such informal chitchat by employment interviewers can be construed by a job applicant as discrimination. Moreover, if interviewers base employment decisions on the fact that the candidate is different, because of appearance, communicative skills, size, or sex, from the employees currently holding these positions, this concept of "different and therefore not as qualified" can be termed discrimination. Proper ways of avoiding these pitfalls will be discussed later in this chapter.

AFFIRMATIVE ACTION

Although few fair-minded persons today would quarrel with the concept of nondiscrimination as applied to the employment of minorities and women, some of these same individuals object quite strenuously to the so-called quota system which has become an important underpinning of affirmative action. In fact, there are important voices being raised in this country to the effect that quotas are contrary to the letter of the 1964 Civil Rights Act. One such voice is that of Senator Daniel P. Moynihan (Democrat, New York), who, as Assistant Secretary of Labor in the administration of Lyndon Johnson, helped draft the implementing executive order on EEO. He notes in his article appearing in the December 1980 issue of *Harper's* magazine that classification by race was not intended. He flatly states, "This was just the sort of thing we assumed we were working against."

The U.S. Supreme Court seems to have had appreciable difficulty interpreting the 1964 Civil Rights Act. In 1978, the Court rendered a markedly split decision in *Regents of the University of California v. Bakke.*[1] In this decision, rigid numerical quotas were declared illegal, but it was suggested that federally aided institutions could take some "notice" of race. This contradiction was resolved a year later when the Court in the *Steelworkers v. Weber* case[2] declared that "voluntary" quotas were indeed legal. In this decision, too, the Court split, and Justice Rehnquist, in a blistering dissent, attacked the majority's opinion as straying far from the truth.

The general confusion that has stemmed from these interpretations would seem to indicate that, as is so frequently the case, the Court is as much concerned with the conceivable social implications of its decisions as it is with a strict interpretation of the law itself. Since Supreme Court justices are human and since the composition of the Court obviously changes from time to time, it is quite conceivable that new and different interpretations of the 1964 Civil Rights Act are still to come.

The authors take the view that there is appreciable merit to the concept that some sort of legal assistance—whether it be quotas or otherwise—must be put into operation if minorities and women

---

[1] U.S. Sup. Ct. (1978) 17 FED Cases 1000.

[2] U.S. Sup. Ct. (1979) 19 FED Cases 1493.

are to achieve their rightful place in industry. Many, but not all, employers today honestly believe that everyone should be treated equally. This concept would be most effective in assuring EEO if we were just starting up our businesses and if all our applicants were starting from an equal footing. However, the reality of the matter is that society as a whole has not provided equal opportunity—not in education, not in employment, not in housing, and not even in government. As a result there is a great backlog of employment inequity in our country. Eliminating this backlog and preventing its repetition are problems confronting employers today, and these problems will not solve themselves. Action is needed to reduce the inequity and eventually to eliminate it. This is the entire purpose of affirmative action.

As noted above, the authors have no real quarrel with affirmative action, so long as such action results in the employment of *qualified* people. But we are strongly opposed to the *indiscriminate* employment of minorities and women solely to fill quotas. In fact, the indiscriminate hiring of minorities and nonminorities alike not only is extremely expensive but also takes huge bites out of productivity. It is a matter of some interest that in the January 25, 1981, edition of *The New York Times* a Japanese car manufacturer made the statement that Japan has a competitive advantage over Detroit because American car manufacturers are forced to hire unqualified minorities.

We believe that there is far too much indiscriminate hiring of both plant and office personnel, primarily because many companies do not have the required expertise. That is what this book is all about. In order to reverse the trend toward indiscriminate hiring, two factors are of great importance: (1) a well-designed selection program that meets all legal tests and (2) trained personnel to operate such a program. Of particular importance is the training of interviewers—persons who make the final employment decision.

What Is Affirmative Action?

Affirmative action is more than nondiscrimination. Whereas nondiscrimination requires, simply, that all discriminatory conditions, whether purposeful or inadvertent, be eliminated, affirmative action requires the employer to make *positive efforts* to recruit, employ, train, and promote qualified minority members and women when it is clear that they have been excluded from jobs in the past, even though no overt or traceable discrimination is evident. If minority members or women have not been employed in numbers that reflect their availability in the area work force, affirmative action is required to recruit and employ proportionately more qualified minority members and women.

Even though an employer may, according to its written policies, be an "equal opportunity employer," it cannot remain "neutral." It must take affirmative action when the employment roster shows that the results of actual hiring, promotion, and job assignment do not reflect the avowed intent of its written policies. Since words alone do not produce jobs or promotions, results—not mere stated intent—are paramount.

Every organization doing business with the government in excess of $100,000 and employing more than 50 people is required by federal regulation to have a written affirmative action program. In such programs, companies are obligated to specify attainable goals and to improve the proportion of minority members and women employed at all levels. Failure to live up to affirmative action programs can result in loss of government contracts, not only in the facility where the failure occurred but in all other operations of the company as well.

An Effective Affirmative Action Program Is Good Insurance

Any company, on its own, can put together an affirmative action program that satisfies federal regulations and, at the same time, is far less expensive than many court-imposed remedies. Most employment people, of course, are familiar with the costly AT&T consent decree of 1973 and the steel industry consent decree of 1974. More recently a consent decree resulting from proceedings against Pacific Southwest Airlines resulted in:

1. $275,000 in back pay
2. An agreement to employ blacks, Hispanics, and men as flight attendants
3. An agreement to abandon selection standards which specified a high school diploma, 2 years of college, and a maximum height of 5 ft 9 in

Likewise, a case involving the Police Department of Los Angeles versus the U.S. Justice Department and five female police officers resulted in:

1. Agreement to a consent decree for minorities and females that included $2 million in back pay
2. Establishment of goals and timetables for hiring blacks and Hispanics in parity with their representation in the metropolitan Los Angeles labor force
3. Ultimate goals for women to represent 20 percent of police ranks
4. Interim goals including 45 percent minority representation in entry-level police jobs and a sliding scale for hiring women, beginning at 20 percent for the first year and climbing to 25 percent until the targeted work force percentage has been reached

It should be clear from the above that court-imposed consent decrees are to be avoided at all costs. To permit a situation to deteriorate to the point where a company becomes vulnerable to a consent decree is not only enormously expensive but also reflective of poor management. To avoid that kind of imposition, then, personnel management must take up the challenge of affirmative action, which really means that it must now do the kind of personnel job that it should have been doing anyway.

Line Supervisors the Key Factor

The question is often raised as to who has the primary responsibility for implementing the affirmative action program. Many supervisors assume, somehow, that "others" are responsible for the success of the affirmative action program—top management, middle management, the personnel manager, the office manager, the equal employment administrator, or their staffs. While these people do have important responsibilities for providing direction, they cannot do the job without the wholehearted support of line supervisors. Because they are closest to the scene of action, line supervisors have the primary responsibility for the success of the affirmative action program. They are the ones who are responsible for making such decisions as:

1. Selecting from among recommended candidates to fill vacancies
2. Determining which employees will be given specific assignments
3. Evaluating employees' performances
4. Deciding which employees will be promoted
5. Deciding which employees will be selected for training and development for higher job assignments

The overall success of the affirmative action program depends on the sum of its implementation in each individual unit. Hence, it is the supervisor's crucial role to make it work in his or her unit. The big picture of an organization's EEO effort is composed of the "little" scenes going on in the work units of individual supervisors. For example, the sales office may have only a handful of vacancies or promotions in a given year, but if this office and other sales offices cumulatively fail to take appropriate affirmative action in the hiring or promoting of minorities and females, then the entire sales organization will have done virtually nothing by the end of the year to promote affirmative action.

It cannot be stressed too strongly that each personnel decision is important because the sum of these decisions makes it obvious to even the most unsophisticated observer whether or not the company is in fact an equal opportunity employer. Results in this area will be obtained in much the same way that all results are accomplished—through the supervisory force. There is no simple rule book to follow, and there are no pat formulas or magic recipes.

The "rules" for EEO and affirmative action are really principles and guidelines, not specific and detailed instructions. A supervisor must exercise good judgment, evaluate situational factors, and try sincerely to be fair and reasonable when applying these principles and guidelines in a particular set of circumstances. For example, not hiring or promoting a minority member to a vacancy may be discriminatory under some circumstances and not in others. The exact circumstances will determine whether discrimination took place or not—the nature of questions asked during the interview, the performance and absentee record of the minority member compared with that of the person hired or promoted, and the number of minority employees hired or promoted to the same or similar jobs in the past. Other things being equal, was the person who was hired or promoted substantially more qualified than the minority member? Was there a goal commitment to hire more minority personnel in the unit? What has been the supervisor's past record in hiring or promoting minorities?

The need for remedial affirmative action can be forestalled or at least minimized by following the equal opportunity principles of employment. Such principles if implemented properly are not incompatible with merit employment. When hiring, assigning, promoting, or training employees, always give minorities, women, and handicapped persons equal opportunity. Give them the same chance given to all others. To do this, it may be necessary for employers to free themselves from subtle attitudes which may subconsciously bias them. They may have to free themselves from stereotyped thinking about the suitability of candidates and to break themselves out of some embedded habits of thought.

The need for corrective affirmative action is always greater when an employer fails to follow equal employment principles. Discrimination can grow because of carelessness and neglect, creating a backlog of problems that are difficult to correct, and failure to correct such problems may invite enforcement of regulations—enforcement that could take the form of consent decrees. As we have seen from examples cited above, consent decrees can take the form of back pay, retroactive seniority, makeup goals, and timetables.

The Office of Federal Contract Compliance Programs (OFCCP), which administers the federal regulations concerning affirmative action, defines affirmative action as those result-oriented actions which a contractor, by virtue of its contracts, must take to ensure equal employment. In addition, contractors are required to have an affirmative action program for the handicapped, disabled veterans, and veterans of the Vietnam era.

ENFORCEMENT OF REGULATIONS

The OFCCP enforces presidential executive orders such as Executive Order 11246 and amendments. In addition to examining whether a contractor meets the technical provisions of the regulations relating to the development and implementation of effective affirmative action compliance programs, the OFCCP directs its main thrust of review toward the statistical analysis of the percentage of minorities and females in a contractor's work force in relation to the availability of minorities and females with the requisite skills in the local area. Failure to comply with regulations of the OFCCP could render a contractor unawardable for federal contracts. The OFCCP basically restricts its reviews to statistical analyses and reviews of large groups or classes of employees or applicants. Its review generally does not involve individual complaints or acts of discrimination. But this agency does investigate class action complaints. Detailed information as to the format and procedures of OFCCP investigations and compliance reviews is contained in the *Federal Contract Compliance Manual—1974.*

Equal Employment Opportunity Commission— State and Local Enforcement Agencies

The Equal Employment Opportunity Commission (EEOC), along with a number of state and local agencies, enforces the provisions of Title VII of the Civil Rights Act of 1964, which are the basic provisions calling for nondiscrimination in all types of employment. Review by these agencies basically involves *individual* cases of discrimination and does not include statistical analyses and review of patterns and practices as is the case with the OFCCP. Remedies sought by these organizations involve back pay for the affected individuals.

Now that we have discussed the concepts of EEO and affirmative action and have pointed out the extent to which companies can get themselves into serious trouble by failing to establish and implement affirmative action programs, let us concentrate on the brighter side of the picture—how to avoid difficulty with the implementation of the regulations and, at the same time, *raise the standards* of the selection program. The chapter that follows discusses a number of time-tested procedures for accomplishing these ends.

CHAPTER THREE

How to Reduce Vulnerability to Government Intervention

As indicated earlier, many companies have become so intimidated by EEO regulations that they have completely abandoned any kind of genuine selection program for entry-level people in the plant and office. The *indiscriminate* hiring that has replaced the previous selection program in such companies not only is unnecessary but also can conceivably launch an organization on the road to bankruptcy. Few companies can survive the practice of indiscriminate hiring—with its attendant high turnover and loss of productivity—over an appreciable period of time. This is all the more true today since, in addition to competing with other American organizations, industry in this country faces the threat of competition from industry in such countries as West Germany and Japan, where the work force is evidently more highly motivated, more efficient, and more stable.

A major reason why many companies have abandoned a genuine selection system—directed at providing the best possible candidates—is *too much emphasis on what EEO regulations prohibit employers from doing*. Emphasis must be placed on *what can be done.* There are a number of steps which companies can undertake—steps that will make it possible for them to build an efficient selection program and, at the same time, satisfy the requirements of EEO regulations. At the outset, though, it should be understood that the recommended procedures discussed in this chapter will not necessarily eliminate all compliance liability. Experience has shown, however, that adoption of the time-tested and common-sense methods discussed here should substantially reduce the likelihood of vulnerability to government intervention.

Rather surprisingly, experience has also shown that adoption of the recommended methods should not only reduce vulnerability to government intervention *but also contribute appreciably to the efficient operation of the entire personnel function.* The latter result represents an unanticipated bonus, but as each of the procedures is discussed below, the existence of this bonus should become abundantly clear. This bonus represents a leavening factor since so many people feel that affirmative action programs are a nuisance—another form of government bureaucracy and something of a "thorn in their sides." As we shall see, however, regulations protecting minorities and females force a company to review its selection methods and to evaluate its entire work force. In so doing, many employers have found that such a review of employees has resulted, among other things, in the discovery of employees with a great deal of potential for movement within the organization. At any rate, the techniques that follow make it possible to select the best-qualified candidates for entry-level jobs and to accomplish this within the framework of EEO regulations.

SCRUTINIZE JOB SPECIFICATIONS AND REQUIREMENTS

Many companies get into trouble because indicated job requirements are not valid in the first place. For example, a job specification may include the requirement that a candidate have a high school education and 2 years of college when, as a matter of fact, many employees now holding such positions and performing them satisfactorily do not have that level of education.

Job orders must be checked to make sure that they do not contain sex preferences—preferences for men or women only. Thus, a job request should not specify 10 men or 4 women. The only instance in which a sex preference can be indicated is one where a bona fide job requirement justifies the exclusion of either a male or female candidate. A male attendant in a men's toilet facility would represent one example of such a bona fide stipulation. An order requesting a man to fill a job that required inordinately heavy lifting would not represent a valid request.

It is sad to say, however, that many interviewers are not sufficiently familiar with job specifications to be able to decide whether a given request is valid or not. Because of inadequate training and often times heavy applicant load, many interviewers have little firsthand information about the jobs they are called upon to fill. If interviewers were to spend perhaps only 1 day a month in the facility learning about the various jobs, they not only would be in a better position to determine the validity of job requests but also should be able to place candidates on jobs that will make the best use of their abilities. This in-depth analysis of jobs will also enable the interviewers to establish a working relationship with line supervision and to become more than a voice on the other end of the telephone in the employment office.

Many companies have job specifications which indicate duties required of the individual who fills a particular job. However, few companies have developed worker specifications which detail the kind of abilities and personality traits required for success on a given job. Over a period of time, interviewers can develop their own specifications by talking with supervisors and employees. Most supervisors have a very good understanding of what it takes to perform satisfactorily on those jobs which they supervise. Talking with employees, with a view to determining what they like best or least about their jobs and what traits or abilities they think are required, can also be productive. A tour of the plant or office helps the interviewer to acquire a better awareness of environmental factors, such as noise, heat, changing conditions, safety hazards, and excessive routine. Specific instruction for developing worker specifications will be found in Chapter 5.

When possible, information ascertained during exit interviews should be reviewed by placement interviewers. From this information the interviewers should be certain that the terminations are not a result of faulty placements made because of unfamiliarity with worker specifications.

Some personnel people do not realize that, as soon as new job orders arrive and have been adequately validated, such openings must be registered with the state employment office. The Vietnam-Era Veterans' Act of 1974, among other things, requires that all job openings under $25,000 be registered with the appropriate state employment office. This specific provision is best implemented by employment interviewers, who are in the best position to monitor the flow of job requests.

It should be clear from the foregoing discussion that EEO regulations, as odious as they sometimes seem, often have the effect of forcing the personnel department to adopt practices which it should have been carrying out all along. In this instance, determining the validity of job requests forces interviewers to get the kind of firsthand information which should enable them to do a far superior selection job. How can interviewers determine the applicants' tolerance to noise, for example, if they don't know the dimensions of the noise factor in a given job situation?

MONITOR APPLICANT FLOW DATA

If a company is to employ an appropriate number of minority and women personnel, it must set up some means of monitoring the number of candidates who appear at the employment office, by race and sex. On the one hand, if the number of minority and women applicants is less then the number needed to meet the affirmative action goals, management must be informed so that an expanded recruitment program can be put into play. On the other hand, if the number of minority and female applications for job openings increases dramatically, affirmative action goals should be raised according to the new availability. For example, if a given company has an affirmative action goal of hiring 10 percent females in a blue-collar job category and the percentage of females applying for such blue-collar jobs consistently remains substantially above 10 percent of the applicants appearing at the employment office, the goal should be adjusted upward in order to avoid adverse impact against females. This example reflects the fact that the number of females hired has to be determined by the percentage of qualified females applying for jobs.

The monitoring of applicant flow data also has a direct bearing on the selection ratio—the number of applicants processed for each candidate deemed "best-qualified" and hired. We have pointed out earlier that at least four or five applicants should be considered before a selection is made. Moreover, if a company can recruit applicants in sufficient number so that it becomes possible to chose one out of every ten who apply, the quality of persons hired should of course improve all the more. Thus, the monitoring of applicant flow impacts upon efficient selection as well as upon affirmative action. It is a necessary device to ensure that a sufficient number of both minorities and nonminorities are processed.

STAY ABREAST OF AFFIRMATIVE ACTION GOALS

A summary of actual placements compared with projected affirmative action goals should be tabulated on a *monthly basis.* If this is not done, companies frequently find themselves in the position of having to "play catch up." Once they fall behind in terms of hiring in accordance with their goals, they are forced into the position of becoming less selective in order to meet such goals. If, at the midyear point, a company suddenly finds that it has hired only 5 percent minority office workers against a projected goal of 10 percent, it may be necessary for that company to employ 20 percent or more minorities during the second half of the year. In most cases, this would mean that, in order to meet the larger numbers needed, that company would have to become less selective.

Getting substantially behind schedule can conceivably place an organization in great financial jeopardy. Government compliance officers may conduct a review of goal attainment at any time during the year. If such officers happen to appear at a time when a given company was appreciably behind schedule, they might take the kind of action that would cost that company a great deal of money.

If goals are not being met because of inadequate numbers of qualified applicants, the personnel department should take immediate action. As a first step, the department must go on record with higher management that it is experiencing difficulty meeting goals. This kind of documentation demonstrates to a reviewing officer that the company is aware of its problems and plans to take remedial action. Remedial action, of course, has to take the form of an expanded recruiting program. The following activities frequently produce good results:

1. Contact minority and female community groups, in an effort to determine whether they can provide assistance in securing additional applicants.

2. Conduct a review of present employees, some of whom may be qualified for higher-level positions than the ones they currently occupy.

3. Provide some kind of bonus to present to employees as a reward for referring qualified candidates.

4. Inform training centers of company needs and suggest plant visitations so that those in charge can get a firsthand understanding of the jobs involved.

All efforts to expand recruitment, whatever they may be, must be carefully documented, in order to show government officials that the company is making every effort to comply with regulations.

There are times when goals are not met even when applicants *are* available. This is often because people responsible for hiring are not fully aware of affirmative action goals. Employment interviewers should be familiar with *all* affirmative action goals. And there are times, of course, when there are not sufficient job openings to absorb the appropriate number of minorities and females. This occurs when the percent of minorities and females applying exceeds affirmative action goals based on prior availability. In this case, it is extremely important to have a written record of why minorities and females are not being hired. Whatever the situation may be, it is important to have an action-oriented program—a program that assures that goals are met or at least that good faith efforts were taken to meet such goals.

MAINTAIN RELIABLE DATA

The three most successful defenses in case of a charge of discrimination are good documentation, good documentation, and good documentation.

Interviewers' and line supervisors' comments must contain clear, concise, job-related reasons for denying an applicant employment or denying an employee a promotion. Otherwise, a company has little chance of winning a case of discrimination. Such reliable documentation should appear on reports of the preliminary interview, the job interview, the exit interview, rating information used for promotion, and recorded results of disciplinary interviews. All such interview comments should be dated and signed.

When questions are directed to the personnel department, management must feel confident that the numbers returned are correct. Once management begins to doubt the accuracy of information supplied by the personnel department, internal credibility is lost. If, for example, personnel records showing the number of applicants hired do not agree with reports showing the number of persons added to the payroll over a given period of time, management as well as government representatives may soon begin to doubt *everything*.

Importance of Dictating Equipment

Because of increased record keeping, we strongly urge the purchase of dictating equipment. Such equipment costs only a few hundred dollars and will pay for itself in a short period of time. If interviewers resist the use of this equipment, managers should *insist* that they learn to use it. Once they have become accustomed to it, they will find it a wonderful time saver. Employment-office records will improve in quality, thoroughness, and timeliness.

KEEP ACCURATE RECORDS ON HANDICAPPED APPLICANTS

The Rehabilitation Act of 1973 requires that employers make special efforts to employ and promote mentally and physically handicapped persons. Handicapped persons have historically experienced difficulty in getting hired. Employers with federal contracts must remove architectural barriers at employment offices to enable the handicapped to apply for jobs. Such contractors must also maintain records on all applicants or employees who, because of a mental or physical problem, cannot be hired, promoted, or transferred.

Records should include not just numbers, but also specific reasons why handicapped persons were not hired and what specific accommodations were considered or made. Records should also show that handicapped people were considered for every job opening for which they were conceivably qualified during the time their application for employment was under active scrutiny.

Many companies have discovered, incidentally, that handicapped persons, properly placed, frequently make extremely valuable employees. Most handicapped people realize that their opportunities for employment are limited. When they do get a job, therefore, they make every effort to keep it. From a psychological standpoint, moreover, many handicapped persons try, perhaps unconsciously, to compensate for their handicap by developing a particularly pleasant personality or by becoming an unusually hard worker.

The affirmative action program for handicapped persons—and for minorities and females as well—requires both annual notification of referral sources that the employer is an equal opportunity employer and the posting of notices throughout the building to that effect. To some companies, this simply means the preparation of a "paper program." They write affirmative action programs containing as many as 30, 40, or even 50 pages of items that will be performed each year. The program is then signed, dated by the manager as an example of the good faith efforts that will be taken, and then put on the shelf since there is no real intention of fulfilling the recruitment, outreach, handicapped procedures, and many other intricate items stated in the program. Such companies may get away with this kind of action for awhile, but they run enormous risks—risks that could conceivably undermine their financial structure.

As pointed out earlier, many companies that initially regarded affirmative action programs as a necessary evil subsequently discover that such programs have their positive aspects. The regulations protecting handicapped persons, minorities, and females force many employers to review their entire work force, in order to assure equal treatment of all employees with regard to promotion. This kind of scrutiny not only meets government requirements but also frequently turns up employees with a surprising amount of potential for upgrading. Women are found in secretarial positions, for example, who over the years have earned additional academic degrees and are completely capable of handling positions on a much higher level. The same situation is often encountered with employees in blue-collar jobs in the plant. As unfortunate as it may seem, a growing number of persons with college educations are taking entry-level jobs in industry because of the marked differential in pay. Teachers earning $15,000 a year are sorely tempted by an entry-level job in industry paying $20,000. Many such persons obviously have potential for subsequent upgrading to a variety of administrative or supervisory positions.

INTERVIEW TERMINATED EMPLOYEES

It has always been a good idea to conduct an in-depth exit interview to explore the reasons why employees leave the company. But now, under EEO, such interviews virtually have become mandatory. If the employee is leaving *voluntarily*, his or her decision may reflect such factors as inappropriate initial selection and placement, ineffective supervision, inappropriate company policies, or low morale in the organization.

The exit interview represents an excellent opportunity to get feedback on the initial hiring decision. Interviewers can learn how efficient or perhaps inefficient they have been in carrying out the selection process. In so doing, they can often profit by their mistakes, resolving perhaps to become tougher-minded in their judgment of people or more realistic in terms of expecting people who have not worked in a blue-collar environment to adjust easily to that type of work situation. In any event, a careful tabulation of the reasons why employees voluntarily give up their jobs can throw considerable light on the whole selection process.

When employees have been *involuntarily* terminated, it is even more essential to review the reasons for separation and to record these clearly and concisely. In order to protect the company from possible discrimination charges, the following two points are extremely important:

1. Make sure that there is a consistent procedure in effect. For example, if it is the company's policy to discharge employees after missing 5 days of work, it should be ascertained whether this policy is being administered strictly or whether there are any employees still on the payroll who have exceeded that limit. This type of scrutiny should be made of all standards.

2. All employees, both hourly and salaried, who have been involuntarily terminated during their probationary period should

have in their personnel folders a letter or other form of documentation from the department stating the precise reason why they have been terminated. Again, a review should be made of these records to determine consistency.

Unfortunately, the review of records of terminated employees frequently amounts to a paperwork exercise only. Rarely do the right people sit down and analyze and use as feedback the results of the termination review. In the case of involuntary terminations, it is imperative that such terminations be reviewed in order to determine whether consistent standards have been applied and whether the reason for discharge can be justified.

KEEP DOCUMENTATION TIMELY

Recording of comments, preparation of reports, and filing of records should be done as close to the time of the event to which they pertain as possible. When, for example, interviewers postpone writing comments on all the applicants they have seen until the end of the day, they often get the various applicants mixed up and, in addition, all their comments tend to sound the same. The delay of report writing until substantially after the event occurs sometimes results in the recording of data that is completely erroneous. Finally, the accumulation of backlogs in filing, of course, results in a subsequent rush job and the usual attendant errors.

Interviewers' comments on applicants who have been hired should show the date of the job offer, the date the applicant is to report for work, the position and department to which the applicant is to be assigned, and some code, such as a numerical system, to tie the hiring of the employee back to the job order.

In the case of those applicants not hired, interviewer comments should show specific and objective reasons for rejecting the individual. All applications should contain "close out" comments such as "hired," "rejected," "did not report for test," or "did not show up for job."

When records are inspected by government personnel and found to be incomplete, the company becomes vulnerable. For example, the organization may be criticized for not hiring older applicants when this may not be the case at all. When interviewers get behind in their record keeping, moreover, they often settle for second-best applicants rather than those best-qualified. A given manager may say, "I need 10 people tomorrow morning." Unfortunately, there is a great tendency for interviewers to hire the next 10 able-bodied people they see, rather than to review the applicants they have already interviewed, many of whom may be far superior. When accurate, timely records do not exist, the personnel department cannot have an efficient operation.

EMPLOY COMMON SENSE AND CONSISTENCY

Personnel departments—like all other departments in an organization—often remain uncritical of their own procedures. As one person recently noted, "People think they should keep doing what they are doing because they have always done it that way, even though it does not make sense." When problems necessitating critical review do occur, all persons concerned are often astonished that the problem resulted from procedures that make no sense at all. Only then do we hear the comment, "If we had only reviewed what we were doing and used some common sense, this would never have happened."

Lack of good common sense is also responsible for the generation of much unnecessary paperwork. And, of course, one piece of unnecessary paper can very easily generate three other pieces. Certainly, it is time that personnel departments turn a critical eye on some of their own methods and procedures.

Whatever the procedure, once it is established, it must be exercised with *consistency*. Again, the company is vulnerable if it treats some of its applicants or employees differently than it does others. A system should be sufficiently flexible that occasional exceptions can be made, but such exceptions must be rare and must be carefully documented. Some companies, for example, have a policy that a given test may not be retaken for a period of 1 year. An exception could conceivably be made here if an applicant could prove that he or she had taken some type of relevant formal training and could therefore be expected to score higher than before. In such a case, it might be possible to permit the retaking of the test after 6 months rather than after a year's wait.

A personnel department should make certain that it can "live with" a given procedure before it is established and set in place.

If it sets up a procedure, for example, whereby no typist will be hired who cannot type 50 words a minute, that department may subsequently discover it cannot find enough typists who can perform at that rate. Or, it may find that the rule precludes the hiring of persons who can type only 40 words per minute but who have other valuable compensating skills.

To cite another example, it seems senseless to establish a rule that no employee can be transferred or promoted during the first 2 years of employment. Such a rule could penalize new employees with unusual potential—employees who might find their entry-level jobs so boring and undemanding that they decide to leave the company.

Normally, consistency and common sense should go hand in hand with efficiency. A good, efficient system will be easy to administer with little need for exceptions, and, in contrast to much current thinking, there is no reason that a good, workable, and sensible system cannot have high standards. There is nothing in any of the regulations that says that standards and procedures cannot be high, so long as they meet a company's needs and goals and so long as they are applied consistently to everybody.

A good formula to follow will take the following shape:

1. Set a goal.
2. Establish procedures that make sense and are fair and that the company can live with.
3. Be consistent.

EXERCISE GOOD PUBLIC RELATIONS

Interviewers, and other members of the personnel department as well, must make every effort to determine that applicants leave the office with a positive impression. Perhaps 90 percent of all people who have contact with a company obtain their only impression of that organization from the company's personnel department representatives. Thus, if someone in personnel has a bad day, is unconsciously rude, or "turns off" an applicant in some way, that applicant leaves with a negative impression of the entire company—because of one person.

It is a psychological put-down to tell people that they are not going to be hired. Many will immediately review their discussion with a view to rationalizing some of the factors in their background which led to their rejection. They may say to themselves—or for that matter to the interviewer—that they are being turned down because they are black, or because they do not have a high school diploma, or because they are too fat. This is the stuff that some cases of discrimination are made of. So, as one expert in the field says, "Don't give them bullets to shoot you down with." It is far better to tell applicants that their qualifications will be compared with those of others who have recently been seen and that the employment office will be in touch with them. This approach gives individuals the feeling that their overall qualifications will receive more consideration, and it does not undermine their sense of self-worth, as a negative approach would.

Should an applicant return to find out why he or she was not hired, the person should simply be told that there were others with qualifications more related to the job. If the applicant *presses* by asking what can be done to improve his or her qualifications, the interviewer should avoid a counseling situation. Most interviewers are not psychologists and hence do not have the background to provide such advice. But they should be familiar with resources in the community and be in a position to refer individuals to the proper place. For example, should the applicant mention trouble formulating career goals, the interviewer could conceivably refer the individual to a local psychologist for vocational guidance.

There are occasions, though, when interviewers may give job-related advice as a matter of good public relations. When, for example, an applicant with a spotty work record and/or poor attendance on prior jobs asks what to do to become more marketable, the interviewer could encourage that applicant to return for reconsideration after he or she has reestablished a stable period of employment. The stable period of employment need not be an excessive period of time but should be a minimum of a year. The applicant who returns for future consideration, after having established a stable period of employment, will come back with a positive image of the company and of the interviewer as well and will have demonstrated some positive personality modification in the areas of motivation and maturity.

Treat Government Investigators
as Fellow Professionals

Good public relations also include relationships with government employees investigating complaints of discrimination and with government compliance officers reviewing the company's EEO status. Experience has shown that an adversary relationship with government investigators is a no-win situation. It is all too easy to fall into the trap of believing that the company is always right and the government is always wrong. Company representatives must remain objective. Investigations and complaints must be viewed on a case-by-case basis and evaluated on their merits. If the company is wrong, the case should be settled as expeditiously as possible. The company's willingness to handle such complaints fairly and efficiently will build a positive relationship with government representatives, and this positive image will also help the company representatives to stand their ground when the company is not at fault. Furthermore, government officers may give the company the benefit of the doubt in close cases or where there is no hard proof either way.

The above recommendations for establishing a positive working relationship with government investigators should in no way be taken as advocating cute shortcuts for getting out of the company's EEO requirements. Personnel people should develop the reputation of fairness and efficiency, rather than play "Philadelphia lawyer."

NEW REAGAN ADMINISTRATION RELAXATION OF JOB BIAS REGULATIONS

The Reagan administration has recently announced long-promised and controversial plans to ease job bias regulations affecting employers who do business with the federal government. These plans reverse a regulatory trend of nearly two decades. But this easing of EEO regulations must not be confused with wiping the slate clean and enabling contractors to take a hard stand against the implementation of EEO regulations. The announced regulatory changes simply eliminate unnecessary paperwork and are designed to create an incentive for voluntary compliance with the regulations. Hence, these changes in no way alter the spirit or intent of EEO regulations.

RECOMMENDED INTERNAL PROCEDURES

Thus far in this chapter we have discussed the adoption of recommended methods that should not only reduce vulnerability to government intervention but also contribute appreciably to the effective operation of the entire personnel function. There are two additional important steps that can be extremely effective:

1. The adoption of an internal complaint handling procedure. This internal process will allow employees to air their complaints to company representatives rather than to government agencies.

2. The implementation of an internal auditing procedure for personnel and EEO self-analysis.

These procedures readily identify problem areas where potential financial liability may exist. They also identify internal problems and enable the company to improve its overall efficiency.

Internal Complaint Procedure

As indicated earlier, many companies spend as much as 40 hours of administrative time alone to handle one charge of discrimination. It is also true that many employees file charges of discrimination with government agencies out of frustration. These two facts by themselves indicate the need for establishing a system aimed at reducing the filing of such charges.

Experience has shown that the appointment of an ombudsman for the purpose of airing employee complaints can effectively reduce charges of discrimination. Whether a company's complaint procedure is formal or informal, it should have the purpose of giving the employees a chance to air their complaints to company representatives rather than filing charges with government agencies. The experience of a number of companies has shown that such an internal complaint procedure has a positive effect on employee morale and, at the same time, often identifies internal problems that require genuine attention. In setting up this internal procedure, companies have found the following steps effective:

1. Employ a companywide ombudsman to coordinate the activities of the in-house complaint handling procedure.

2. Appoint area EEO representatives. If the facility is large enough, a representative should be appointed for each depart-

ment. These area representatives have the function of assisting the ombudsman in getting the facts.

3. Notify employees about the in-house complaint handling procedure and inform them that they should discuss any complaints of possible discrimination or other work-related problems with the company's internal ombudsman. Employees should be assured of nonretaliation and given freedom to discuss the problems during normal working hours.

4. When employees visit the ombudsman, they should be encouraged to state their problems frankly. The ombudsman will then determine the nature of the complaint, gather as many facts as necessary, and advise the employees that a response will be available within a week of the initial meeting.

5. The ombudsman should then contact the area affirmative action representative to ascertain additional details. The complaint should be discussed with higher management and a resolution determined within the promised time frame. All employee complaints must be answered, whether the response is positive or negative.

6. The internal complaint procedure must be result-oriented, and every effort must be made to help the ombudsman establish creditability with the work force.

Investigation has shown that frustration and poor communications represent the basic causes of most employee complaints to outside agencies. Because they have no viable internal recourse, employees go outside, registering their complaints with government agencies. Perhaps because the internal complaint procedure discussed above provides irritated employees with an escape valve, the results are often extremely positive. In one company, for example, the number of charges being filed with outside agencies was reduced by as much as 75 percent.

In addition to reducing the liability and expense involved in handling charges of discrimination, an internal complaint procedure also enables plant management to monitor the heartbeat of the operation and take the necessary corrective action. In this way, it is often possible to attack the problem in the early stages. It is a matter of some interest that a number of companies with nonunion shops have found the internal complaint procedure a useful tool in avoiding unionization.

As implied above, improved administrative procedures often result from the identification of problems by dissatisfied employees. Actually, an informal plant complaint handling procedure can have the same positive effects as an effective employee suggestion device, but much of the success of this program depends upon the selection of the ombudsman. If the ombudsman cannot establish rapport with employees and cannot establish overall creditability with the work force, the entire program can easily fail. Creditability often depends on tangible results.

Internal Personnel and EEO Self-Analysis

Many companies have found a self-analysis of their personnel and EEO policies to be very effective. This early-detection device enables companies to identify potential areas of financial liability. The analysis also permits companies to take the necessary corrective actions if practices and procedures are not in compliance with federal regulations. As noted earlier, federal regulations dealing with EEO require contractors to make good faith efforts toward equal employment. Obviously, an internal self-analysis program that enables a company to identify problems and correct them represents an excellent example of good faith efforts. It should be noted further that self-imposed corrective action will often enable contractors to convince government representatives that they are taking the necessary corrective action and that government intervention is therefore not necessary.

Representatives other than those in the personnel department at the facility in question should perform the internal reviews. In a small company, the review can be conducted by administrative personnel from other departments. In a large company with more than one operation, reviews should be made either by corporate representatives or by personnel representatives from other facilities. Internal reviews help to ensure compliance with government regulations, reduce financial liability, improve management policies and procedures, and enable companies, themselves, to put their houses in order. They also have a further positive impact—that of providing a thorough analysis of current administrative procedures. When personnel people spend a number of years working at one location, they often become so comfortable with current administrative procedures that they are not at all critical of what they are doing. A representative from another department or facility, therefore, can take a more objective look at personnel practices with a view to determining their efficiency. During the course of administering the audit, reviewers should be careful not to indicate their opinion of responses and should continue to be positive when gathering information.

Reviews should be done the same way the government would do them. As a matter of fact, internal reviews are often done better and more thoroughly than those conducted by the government representative. At any rate, having submitted to company internal reviews, personnel people are in excellent shape to go through an actual government review.

All internal reviews, whether conducted at major corporations or small one-company facilities, should have three goals:

1. The review should be conducted to determine whether the company is in compliance with EEO regulations. Even if the company is not a federal contractor and therefore is not subject to requirements of executive orders, it may come under requirements of state or local laws affecting personnel practices and procedures. Hence, the overall goal should be to determine the extent to which a company is in compliance with appropriate laws and whether any potential financial liability exists.

2. The second purpose of the review should be to determine whether or not the facility is following practices and procedures outlined by upper management. Such practices and procedures should include the extent to which employees are being hired in accordance with the company's selection practices, whether they are being paid in accordance with the salary administration program, and whether the current benefit program is being administered properly.

3. The review should also determine whether or not any revisions are necessary or appropriate in current administrative procedures. Recommendations stemming from the review often reveal opportunities for improving efficiency, such as the elimination of unnecessary paperwork.

All of this encourages upper management to have a much more receptive view toward internal personnel and EEO analyses. Without this positive aspect of the review system, upper management, as well as the personnel people involved, see the work resulting from such projects as being counterproductive. The reviewer should question personnel people concerning their ideas for improving efficiency, and ideas of merit should be reported to upper management.

The following represents a detailed internal personnel and EEO audit checklist:

1. *Employment office.*

   a. What are the race, sex, education, experience, qualifications, and training of all employment-office personnel on file?

   b. Are adequate records maintained relating to applicants and new employees by race, sex, and EEO-1 category to permit review of action taken? In particular, is a tally kept which reflects the race, sex, and any test scores achieved by applicants who were rejected for employment?

   c. Are new employees hired on the basis of qualifications, and has the employment manager been given sole authority for hiring new employees for entry-level production, maintenance, and clerical positions and instructed the interviewers accordingly?

      (1) Does the manager exercise that authority?

      (2) Do the interviewers follow the policies of the employment manager?

      (3) Do the interviewers who assign applicants to particular jobs adequately document the reasons for making hiring decisions? Are the comments dated and signed?

      (4) Is an affirmative action effort being made to integrate departments currently predominantly staffed by one race or sex? How?

   d. Is each department required to submit documentation of reasons for returning anyone to the employment office for termination as an unsatisfactory employee during the probationary period or for reassignment in the case of a transferred employee?

   e. If apprenticeship opportunities exist, have appropriate criteria for selection of individuals been made?

      (1) Have steps been taken to inform state employment

service offices and minority-group referral sources of apprenticeship opportunities?

(2) What efforts are made to extend apprenticeship opportunities to minority-group members?

(3) How many of the present apprentices are members of minority groups?

(4) Are there any present apprentices who were accepted into the program despite the fact that they failed to qualify under the announced standards of acceptance? If so, are any of them members of minority groups?

f. Are females being employed by applying standards that have been applied to men? How many women are now employed and in what jobs?

2. *Management responsibility.*

  a. Attention given to employment matters.

  (1) How many conferences have there been with the manager to discuss employment and EEO matters?

  (2) What reports and other documentation of the implementation of the EEO program are provided to management? Are supervisors informed of affirmative action goals?

  b. Attention given to employee complaints.

  (1) Have any personnel- or EEO-related grievances been filed during the last 12 months? What was the issue and disposition of each grievance?

  (2) Have any discrimination charges been filed with government agencies during the last 12 months? What was the issue and disposition of each? Is there a pattern or common complaints in all charges?

  (3) What internal action is management taking to reduce or resolve complaints relating to personnel or EEO?

  (4) Who has the responsibility for resolving complaints?

  c. Distribution of affirmative action programs.

  (1) Have all employment interviewees been informed of EEO obligations and affirmative action goals?

  (2) Have copies of affirmative action programs been dis-

tributed to appropriate members of management for implementation of these programs?

(3) Has top management endorsed the programs? Date and type of endorsement?

3. *Tests.*

   a. What tests are used?

      (1) Identify the tests and the jobs for which the various tests are used. Are the tests specifically related to the necessary qualifications for the particular job?

      (2) Are the tests published or "homemade" tests? If homemade, were the tests professionally developed on the basis of specific job-related criteria? What were the professional qualifications of the designer of any homemade tests?

      (3) What are the dates on which the tests were first used and dates of any changes in tests or test batteries.

   b. Test administration.

      (1) Who administers the tests?

      (2) What are the professional qualifications of the test administrator and the administrator's supervisor?

   c. Test validation.

      (1) Have the tests been validated by careful job analysis to determine that they reflect the required skills and qualifications?

      (2) Has the sample population or norm used in validating the preemployment test included representatives of any minority groups likely to take the test?

      (3) If the tests have not been validated, is a program of validation under way?

      (4) What are the target dates for completion of validation studies on the various tests?

   d. Passing scores.

      (1) Identify the present, and all past, cutoff scores for passing the various tests, the dates on which the scores were established, and the respective tests that were involved. Have any employees who failed the tests

been hired? If so, identify by race, date of testing, and test.

(2) Who determines and, in the past, has determined what constitutes a passing score? On what basis were these determinations made? Are employees who have failed a test given an opportunity to be retested? Have they been retested in the past?

(3) Are test scores divulged to the division or department to which an employee is assigned? If so, why?

e. Are all job applicants tested and, if not, why? Are they given the same tests and, if not, why? If a test is required for transfer to a particular department, has such a test been uniformly administered and graded? Have any employees been allowed to transfer without passing the test? If so, identify by race.

f. Practices on retention of testing records.

4. *Review of affirmative action programs.*

a. Does the facility or an affiliated facility currently hold any government contracts? Dollar amount? Government agency?

b. Do affirmative action programs meet technical provisions outlined in executive orders (and specific provisions outlined in the OFCCP compliance manual)? What goals have been met? What goals have not been met and why?

c. Is the operation able to prepare necessary statistical reports to show that the affirmative action program goals are being monitored? Is adverse impact being analyzed? What did analysis indicate? Was corrective action required?

d. Are all jobs openings under $25,000 being registered with state job services?

e. Have architectural barriers been removed to allow handicapped persons to apply for employment?

f. Is supportive data available to show recruitment efforts to attract minority and female applicants?

g. What are the net results of the facility's affirmative action efforts?

h. Have efforts been taken to establish a committee to review promotions to ensure nondiscrimination? How is the committee constituted? Are records made of meetings so as to document efforts to promote qualified candidates and explain shortcomings of candidates not considered for promotion.

5. *Employee interviews.*

a. What is the general attitude of a cross section of current employees relative to the facility's hiring practices?

b. What is the opinion of the quality of new employees? Do the employees believe that the interviewers understood worker specifications? Does upper management agree with this opinion?

c. What is the general opinion of a cross section of employees toward the company?

d. Do employees know about EEO requirements? Are their feelings negative or positive?

e. Do present employees know how to resolve their own complaints within the company?

6. *Work force statistics.*

a. Compare current company work force statistics for blue-collar, clerical, and management employees by department or work units with the same information 12 months ago. Any trends? Improvement? Negative growth?

The exact procedures to follow when conducting an internal analysis vary greatly, but experience has shown that the checklist shown above represents an effective method for the gathering of internal data.

This checklist method is most effective during the first analysis. After the first review, reference can be made to the basic documented problem areas for further analysis. For example, if the data-gathering checklist indicates lack of proper training of employment interviewers, appropriate recommendations to correct that deficiency should be made during the follow-up visits. The entire data-gathering checklist need not be completed on the initial visit, and areas considered in good shape on the first visit need not be checked again unless changes have occurred.

It is essential that top management of the company be made aware of the results of the data-gathering processes. After information has been gathered and corrective action recommended, the facility should be given 6 months to 1 year to implement the corrective action. Follow-up visits should be made to determine whether such action has been taken. Detailed records of internal analyses and recommended corrective action should be on file and be available, if required, for review by government representatives.

A note of caution is appropriate, however. Long, detailed lists of potential liabilities, when given to government representatives, may become exhibit A and used against the organization. While every effort should be made to make recommendations as specific as possible, this information should be regarded as confidential and not available for public distribution. A company may very well get into a "Catch-22" situation with the recorded results of internal reviews. On the one hand, if information is not sufficiently specific, personnel and management representatives will not be able to understand the recommendations and implement them properly. On the other hand, if information is too specific and self-incriminating, such information can be used against the company. Hence, an organization must use extreme care in terms of what information it chooses to make available to government representatives.

CHAPTER FOUR

Affirmative Action in Operation

Although EEO regulations do not require an employer to hire people who are not qualified, they do specify that minorities, females, and other members of protected groups must be afforded the same *equality of opportunity* that has been offered to other candidates in the past. Much of the current literature on this subject involves lists of dos and don'ts designed to help interviewers thread their way through the intricacies of the regulations. But these lists fail to give interviewers a proper understanding of the spirit and intent of the regulations.

In the past, many interviewers have used an applicant's race, sex, or physical handicap as a criterion for screening the applicant *out* of further consideration. In so doing, they have often based their hiring decisions on surface impressions or snap judgments rather than upon hard data—factual evidence gleaned from an applicant's work history and education. Simply because minorities and females are "different" from candidates who have been hired in the past for certain jobs, they have been impulsively categorized as *not equal* to employees currently filling those jobs. In their efforts to screen out minorities, females, and handicapped persons, some companies have actually used the medical department toward this end, encouraging the company doctor to erect such artificial barriers as size, height, weight, and medical history.

Instead of screening *out* members of protected groups, the emphasis now becomes one of making every effort to screen *in* as many members of such groups as fulfill the job requirements. As suggested in an earlier chapter, this often involves a rather complete change of attitude on the part of interviewers. Instead of being concerned with surface impressions, they are now charged with the responsibility of looking beyond such impressions to discover hard, factual evidence of an individual's ability to perform a job.

Surface Impressions Are Often Unfair and Counterproductive

Some employers report that minority candidates who possess the appropriate technical background and educational requirements are sometimes screened out because they are "quiet, withdrawn, and without leadership potential." This is a mistake, in the first place, because many jobs do not require an outgoing personality or, in fact, leadership skills. It is a mistake, in the second place, to assume that behavior during the interview is necessarily typical of a candidate's behavior in general. Any person being interviewed for a job is understandably nervous and on edge. In addition to this normal concern, minority candidates may be in a strange environment—an environment that may be composed almost entirely of nonminorities. Hence, it is quite understandable that minority candidates may be a little more apprehensive than nonminority candidates about trying to be assertive in the context of an interview. As we shall see in Part 3 of this book, however, it is possible to train interviewers in such a way that they become truly expert in developing rapport with all applicants—to the extent that the candidate's behavior during the interview becomes much more typical of his or her behavior in general.

In their attempts to screen in as many qualified females as possible, interviewers are advised to search for creative ways for recruiting women to fill jobs traditionally held by men. In a case that wonderfully illustrates this point a company involved in the marine industry had been experiencing difficulty finding females to fill traditional male positions in the various crafts throughout the shipyard. This stemmed largely from the fact that employment interviewers at this location reported an inability to find female applicants who possessed the necessary skills or abilities and hence rejected most of them for employment. But one interviewer at this location reasoned that many of the craft positions in the marine industry resembled duties that would be performed by persons interested in sailing. That interviewer reviewed applications of females, looking specifically for individuals with a background or interest in sailing. Female candidates with such an interest or background were brought back for a second interview for the purpose of identifying those individuals with specific experience in tying knots, painting, and preparing boats for repair. As a consequence, a considerable number of women with a background and experience in sailing have been employed at this facility at the entry level and, at this point, are doing very well.

THE HANDICAPPED

The Rehabilitation Act of 1973, requiring the employment of the mentally and physically handicapped, was originally intended for the visibly handicapped—persons whose handicaps others could see, such as wheelchair patients and amputees. In addition to these people, however, there is also in our society a large sector of people who have other medical problems that have historically denied them employment or promotional opportunities. Since these medical problems cannot be seen and hence are unrecognized, this sector of society is now being termed the "silent majority." As a consequence, there has been some confusion concerning the definition of handicapped. Some sectors of our society believe that only obviously handicapped persons (wheelchair patients and amputees) are genuinely handicapped. Others believe that any person with a physical problem—even as minute as wearing glasses—is handicapped. State and federal regulations generally define a handicapped person as anyone with a known disability, a disability that substantially limits his or her life activities. Thus, if an applicant is denied a job because of a physical or mental problem, then this applicant would be handicapped. If an employee is denied a promotion or transfer to a job because of a physical or mental problem, then this employee would be clearly handicapped. This is a functional definition and seems far more accurate than the definition that limits the word "handicapped" to those with physical problems that can actually be seen.

Historically, people with physical problems have been denied employment because of two principal reasons: (1) the thought that other workers unaccustomed to working with the visibly handicapped might experience some discomfort and (2) the belief that persons with a history of medical problems were poor risks with respect to insurance and workers' compensation costs. As a matter of interest, in past years many companies employed physicians for the purpose of screening out handicapped applicants with a history of medical problems. In some companies, in fact, employment interviewers administered medical questionnaires and denied employment to applicants believed to show a likelihood of increasing insurance or compensation costs. It is a small wonder, then, that new regulations were required to correct this injustice.

The Rehabilitation Act of 1973 requires employers to invite applicants or employees to indicate their interest in being covered under the company's affirmative action program for the handicapped and for disabled veterans. But whether or not an applicant or employee indicates a wish to be covered becomes a moot issue once that applicant or employee has been denied employment or a promotion because of a physical problem. Federal regulation requires that such people are subsequently to be considered handicapped.

Screening In the Handicapped

The first thing to remember in processing the handicapped is the fact that interviewers are not trained physicians. They, therefore, should not discuss an applicant's medical problems or history and should not make any medical evaluation as to whether the applicant can or cannot perform the job. If there is any question in the interviewer's mind as to whether a given applicant can physically perform the work—or if applicants ask specific questions as to the nature of the work to be performed—it is the interviewer's job to spell out the nature of the job duties and environmental factors (climbing, working in confined areas, working around heat and fumes). The applicant should then be told that if he or she believes there would be a problem performing those duties because of physical reasons, those problems should be discussed with the doctor.

The question of an applicant's mental or physical ability to perform the job duties must be determined by a physician properly trained in occupational medicine and board-certified. As in the case of employment interviewers, it is also essential that company physicians take the time to observe workers on their jobs in the plant or office. In one case a company physician did not perform any medical duties at all during his first 30 days of employment. Rather, he spent this time familiarizing himself with job and worker specifications and making plant visitations. His familiarization involved not only the actual observation of jobs but also an orientation period with the safety department, the environmental engineers, and the industrial engineers. Because this physician oriented himself to the needs of the company and the worker specifications, he added an entire new dimension to his ability to perform his job. Even in the case of small companies utilizing contract physicians or clinics, such contract physicians should take the time to familiarize themselves with the company's operations and to get a firsthand view of all the jobs in that organization.

The placement of handicapped persons and the implementation of reasonable accommodations to make their employment possible require a team effort. This team effort is usually performed by the physician and the employment interviewer. At times, though, safety specialists, industrial engineers, and environmental health engineers should also be consulted in an effort to explore creative ways of employing the physically and mentally handicapped.

Many companies have discovered that the new policy of screening handicapped persons in rather than out represents a rather difficult transition. For one thing, it now becomes necessary to develop a specific set of medical restrictions or dimensions of an individual's handicap. These dimensions must be clear, concise tools issued by trained medical personnel and rationally interpreted by interviewers. Interviewers are then in a position to make reasonable accommodations and place handicapped persons in jobs which they can safely handle. Although the specifics of such dimensions of course vary in each situation, some examples are listed below. It will be noted that these dimensions give an employment interviewer a clear, concise picture of what the applicant can and cannot do.

1. No repetitive bending, lifting, straining, or pulling in excess of 80 pounds. The key word here is "repetitive." The applicant may do normal lifting below 80 pounds.

2. No working around open pits or moving machinery or on walkways without protective railings. The employee may perform a full range of clerical or production duties not involving the above areas, with the understanding that under no circumstances shall that employee work alone.

The employment interviewer, armed with job descriptions and worker specifications, can now consider applicants relative to their handicapped dimensions. Clearly, there will be jobs that some applicants cannot perform. In those cases, the applicants' applications should remain on file for subsequent consideration when jobs that they *can* perform come to the interviewer's attention. When such a job opening occurs, the interviewer should get the physician's medical opinion as to whether or not the applicant can meet the particular requirements of the job in question. In the final analysis, it is the interviewer's overall responsibility to make the evaluation of the applicant's employability. Once handicapped dimensions have been issued by the medical department and reviewed by the employment interviewer, records should be kept in the handicapped applicant's file of all job vacancies that occur, the accommodations that were considered in order to make the handicapped applicant employable, and the specific reason for denial of employment. These records should be kept for the active life of the applicant's employment inquiry.

Making Job Accommodations
for the Handicapped

When reasonable accommodations can be made to employ a handicapped person, both the individual and the company are likely to emerge as winners. It is a matter of record that handicapped employees miss less time, can be trained to perform the full scope of job duties, and become a real asset to their organization. Because they have fewer options than most of us, they feel fortunate indeed to get a job. And it becomes a matter of pride to demonstrate that their performance is just as good as, perhaps even better than, that of their peers.

In one case several years ago, a company was considering the employment of a deaf and dumb keypunch operator. The keypunch applicant successfully passed the keypunch operator test, was able to meet all preemployment requirements, and was eventually employed as a keypunch operator—with one minor accommodation. Because of a concern for her safety, a warning light was attached to her keypunch machine—a light that would warn her when the fire alarm system was activated. Over a period of several years now, this deaf and dumb keypunch operator has had the lowest absentee record and the highest accuracy record of any keypunch operator in the company. Moreover, she is very satisfied in a job that is to the majority of people very boring, tiresome, repetitive, and noisy. The company has benefited greatly from the contributions of a loyal, efficient, and faithful employee. This case highlights the value of making accommodations where handicapped persons are concerned. If such an accommodation had not been made in this case, an extremely valuable employee would have been lost.

OTHER CONSIDERATIONS IN PROCESSING MEMBERS OF PROTECTED GROUPS

In like manner, applicants with only one eye may be expected to have initial difficulty operating mobile equipment. However, with some extra orientation, they might find themselves completely able to handle the job. In assigning such persons to the operation of mobile equipment, however, it must be determined that the safety of others will not be jeopardized. The interviewer must ask herself or himself this key question: "Can this employee, with additional orientation or training, *safely* perform this job?" A fine line must be drawn between creative, result-oriented ways to employ the handicapped and efforts which endanger the safety of the handicapped employee as well as other workers. Happily, in most situations, the safety problem can be resolved. Modern technology has developed such safety devices as "dead man" controls, and, when similar modifications are made to equipment, handicapped persons can often be employed.

Not only do some females, minorities, older applicants, and

handicapped people have a difficult time relating to some interviewers, some interviewers have a difficult time communicating through the color barrier, the sex barrier, or the generation gap. Interviewers who find themselves in this situation must learn to bridge these gaps or be counted out as professionals. The key to the problem here is *empathy*. Professional interviewers make a conscious effort to "put themselves in the other person's shoes," trying in every way to identify the individual's concerns, fears, and needs. Applicants immediately sense this kind of rapport and respond accordingly, providing a great deal more information about themselves than might otherwise have been the case. Once empathy has been established, moreover, interviewers should concentrate on relevant, factual evidence, rather than on what the person looks like or how he or she communicates. By "relevant, factual evidence" we mean such factors as history of stability (good absenteeism record, not a job-hopper), appropriate education and work experience to conform with worker specifications, evidence of willingness to work, ability to get along with people, and the like. Concentration on empathy, moreover, helps interviewers to avoid a "mechanical" approach to the selection interview. When one interviews a number of individuals in a single day, one must remember that he or she is dealing with human beings, each of whom is a unique individual. When an interviewer's approach becomes mechanical, this fact is subtly communicated to the applicant and not only inhibits communication but may even invite hostility.

Handling Difficult Applicants

Some applicants come in with a chip on their shoulders. Perhaps they have just been turned down for other jobs and have the feeling that they are going to be rejected once again. Interviewers should not permit themselves to be intimidated by such individuals. Rather, they should try all the harder to develop rapport (using techniques discussed in Part 3) and should try to conduct the interview in a completely professional manner. A good interviewer *never* shows surprise or irritation.

In the case of problem individuals, it is important not to invite information of a personal nature that may not be work-related. Above all, try not to provide applicants with opinions or to help them by giving unsolicited advice.

INDUSTRY'S ROLE IN AFFIRMATIVE ACTION TRAINING

Since all of industry is interested today in screening in as many qualified minorities and females as possible, it behooves us all to search for such persons who are *potentially qualified*. By this we mean persons who have what it takes to make a basically good employee but who do not possess the kind of *skills* required. Before trying to do anything in the way of training with these people, we must first decide if they have a reasonable degree of motivation, maturity, and mental ability. If this is not done as an important first step, many individuals enrolled in costly training programs will certainly fall by the wayside.

Internal Training Programs

Many companies today will have already developed internal programs designed to provide minorities, women, the handicapped, and older people with the kinds of skill required for job effectiveness in their organizations. Where such programs are not already in place, management should give serious consideration to the establishment of programs of this kind. Individuals introduced into training programs are counted toward affirmative action goals and thus help to improve the contractor's overall minority profile. As indicated in Chapter 6, moreover, companies may send applicants for training programs to the state employment offices for aptitude testing. Such test results will help immeasurably in determining the extent to which the individual has sufficient mental ability, mathematical aptitude, or mechanical comprehension.

The steel and automotive industries have developed training centers designed to equip newly employed persons lacking experience with the necessary skills for such jobs as electrical and mechanical helpers, machinists, welders, pipe fitters, and computer operators. The trainees receive their instruction on company time, and some of them spend as much as 2 years in such programs. In most centers of this kind, the training is divided between classroom work and on-the-job apprenticeship with a skilled craft worker. These programs are equally effective for people without experience and older individuals who have lost their jobs through plant closings or the effects of automation.

An example of the recycling of employees affected by automation can be found in the experience of the U.S. Post Office. When the U.S. Postal Service introduced automatic mail handling, letter carriers and sorters whose jobs were eliminated by the new automated equipment were retrained as mechanics to service the new equipment. This huge operation was accomplished in such a way that not a single employee had to be fired. Both the postal service and its employees gained in this situation. The employees saved their jobs, and the postal service saved valued employees, employees who were already familiar with the system and had established good employment records.

Community Training Centers

In the case of companies which perhaps are not of sufficient size to establish their own internal training programs, a rather wide variety of community training centers probably represents the answer. In any sizable community there may be as many as 25 or 30 such centers, some of which are funded by the government and are therefore free. In addition, many of the public schools and community colleges provide evening vocational training courses such as typing, sheet metal working, computer programming, and supervisory training.

Personnel people who discover applicants with appropriate potential but without the necessary skills should direct such applicants to area training institutions. If they think well enough of them, moreover, they should monitor their progress from time to time and encourage them to reapply to the company when they have completed their training. This is another example of the manner in which interviewers can utilize creative methods to hire more female and minority personnel.

On-the-Job Orientation

When worker specifications indicate hazardous environmental conditions such as climbing in excess of 25 feet, lifting and bending in confined areas, and operating mobile equipment, interviewers must show particular concern for applicants who have never been subjected to this type of activity. The interviewer's first reaction might be to reject such applicants, but there is another way to approach such inexperience. Some companies are experimenting with "trial periods," where they might, for example, give a woman several days to become familiar with some such hazards. Although perhaps frightened at first, an inexperienced female may find that she can become accustomed to climbing and that, after a day or two, it is no longer a problem. In like manner, employees with only one eye may be expected to have initial difficulty operating mobile equipment, but with some extra orientation might find themselves completely able to handle the job and handle it safely. A key point to remember in employing the handicapped is not to underestimate an applicant's ability to do the job. A key question is, "Can this employee, with additional orientation or training, safely perform the job?" As stated earlier, a fine line must be drawn between creative, result-oriented ways to employ the handicapped and situations which jeopardize the safety of both the handicapped employee and other workers. Usually the safety problem can be resolved.

The Older Worker

Some older workers, bored with early retirement, are returning to the labor market. The interviewer's first impulse might be to reject such older applicants for a wide variety of jobs—particularly those, for example, that involve heavy lifting. But interviewers should be reminded here of the sound psychological principle of *individual differences.* While there are many people in their sixties who would find certain jobs very difficult, there are always others of similar age who could handle those jobs quite easily. We all know of certain older people who are both physically and mentally much younger than their chronological age. President Ronald Reagan would seem to be one such person. How many people of his age would even be interested in shouldering the responsibilities of his office? Therefore, when interviewers encounter older applicants who look younger than their age and who seem to be in unusually good physical and mental condition, they should consider giving such persons an on-the-job trial period. With additional orientation and training, some of these older applicants might very well qualify for some physically demanding jobs. The issue of special orientation or training is critical. Many applicants—young, old, black, white, male, female, handicapped, and nonhandicapped—who on the surface appear unable to do the job or meet worker specifications have proved to be productive, reliable employees if given additional orientation and training to compensate for apparent shortcomings. By doing a better job of selection and by acquiring a better understanding of human behavior, some interviewers have been able to "make a silk purse out of a sow's ear." From a pool of applicants who, on the surface, did not appear to have appropriate qualifications, they have employed many truly productive workers—by assigning such applicants to special orientation and training.

In the beginning of this chapter we talked about industry's responsibility for providing equality of opportunity. Because equality of opportunity has not always been part of American life, affirmative action is now necessary to close the gap. Industry has an obligation to do everything possible for those people who have somehow or other been passed by. The "everything possible" might take the form of (1) split shifts for wives and husbands, (2) flex time, i.e., a work schedule established by the individual employee, based on his or her own preferred hours for working, but totaling a prescribed number of hours per week, or (3) special time off for nursing mothers.

PART TWO

The Selection Process: Its Development and Application

CHAPTER FIVE

Worker Specifications

Just as the *job description* represents a basic tool for salary deter-
mination, so should *worker specifications* form the basis of a good
selection program. Most companies have a set of job descriptions
—descriptions which provide a detailed account of what an employee is required to do on any given job. Few organizations,
however, have taken the trouble to develop worker specifications
—the traits or abilities required for successful performance on a
given job. Yet such delineation is absolutely fundamental to the
development of any selection program. How can an interviewer
evaluate the qualifications of an applicant without knowing what
to look for? Moreover, information contained in worker specifications should provide the basis for the development of the application, the preliminary interview, employment tests, and the
employment interview itself.

We have previously recommended that interviewers spend
some time in the plant or office familiarizing themselves with
working conditions, physical demands, promotional possibilities,
occupational hazards, and other factors of the work setting. They

should also obtain the views of plant management, supervisors, and the hourly workers themselves. In this connection, the authors have recently carried out some 250 interviews with management, supervisors, and hourly employees in a manufacturing organization. The results of these interviews have shown that the essential characteristics of a good employee can be divided into five major categories as follows:

1. Good motivation
    a. Self-starter
    b. High level of work output
    c. Conscientious
        (1) High quality of work
        (2) Good attendance
2. Reasonable mental capacity
    a. Able to learn quickly
    b. Able to plan
    c. Attentive
3. Emotional maturity
    a. Willing to stay with the job—not a job-hopper
    b. Willing to work under basic plant conditions that might involve shift work, heat, noise, and other hazards
    c. Safety-conscious
4. Ability to get along with others
    a. Cooperative
    b. Not a troublemaker
5. Physical capability
    a. Able to lift, climb, stoop, and reach

The above, then, represent so-called common denominator factors that we would like to have in *all* employees. But, in selecting an individual for a specific job, interviewers need to know the *unique* characteristics or abilities required for success on that particular job. Such characteristics and abilities form the substance of the worker specifications.

The development of worker specifications may at first appear to be a monumental job. Although any given operation may have several hundred different jobs, the number of basic entry-level positions for hourly workers is usually quite small. Logically, then, worker specifications should first be developed for those entry-level positions—positions for which most of the hiring from outside sources will be done. Worker specifications should then be developed for other positions that may be filled by more highly skilled applicants as openings in these positions occur.

BUILDING WORKER SPECIFICATIONS

As a first step in building worker specifications for a specific position, interviewers should study the job description. As a second step, they should study applicant data and other background information of incumbents on that job, in an effort to determine unique experience, training, and specific skills. They will then be ready to visit the plant in order to observe the job in question and talk with the supervisor and individual workers. The worker specification questionnaire shown below will serve as a useful guide for organizing the desired information.

WORKER SPECIFICATION QUESTIONNAIRE

_____   _____
Position title   Interviewee

_____   _____
Location   Date

1. *Required aptitudes:* What types of aptitudes are required for the job?

   Verbal _____

   Numerical _____

   Mechanical _____

   Finger dexterity _____

   Manual dexterity _____

   Clerical speed and accuracy _____

   Other _____

2. *Mental ability:* What interpretation, selection, and analysis is required for the job? Is planning necessary? Do mental skills involve judgment and ingenuity?

(continued)

3. *Preemployment training:* What specific training is required?

4. *Employment training and experience:* Once the employee is hired, what training and experience are necessary for the average employee to become proficient in performing the job? How long does it take the average employee to absorb the training and experience?

5. *Responsibility for performance and materials:* How closely is the employee supervised? What materials are involved?

(continued)

6. *Responsibility for contacts:* To what degree are poise, cooperation, and tact required in maintaining good working relationships? Is the employee required to communicate with coworkers only or with the general public as well, directly or by telephone?

_____

_____

_____

_____

_____

7. *Responsibility for direction of others:* How many people does an incumbent in this job supervise? Does this person have disciplinary responsibility?

_____

_____

_____

_____

_____

8. *Working conditions:* What are the general working conditions? Are safety hazards a factor? To what degree are there any disagreeable environmental factors?

_____

_____

_____

_____

_____

9. *Other required characteristics:*

_____

_____

_____

_____

(continued)

_____

Reviewer   Date

As an aid to interviewers who are anxious to develop their own worker specifications, we have prepared job descriptions and worker specifications for two jobs, keypunch operator and machinist (see below). After studying the job description, prepared by the company's industrial engineers, we reviewed background data on five incumbents in each of these job. This analysis included a general overview of each individual's prior work record and education background as well as a review of the strengths and weaknesses which were developed during the employment interview. Interviews were then carried out separately with individual workers and their immediate supervisors. During the course of these interviews, those individuals concerned were informed of the purpose of the project and told that the authors were trying to determine overall unique characteristics for success on that job. They were asked to concentrate not on the characteristics which we would like to have in all employees, such as loyalty, integrity, willingness to work, and ability to get along with others. Rather, they were asked to describe those qualifications that would differentiate their job from other jobs within the organization. The nine major items appearing on the worker specifications questionnaire were reviewed with each individual and their responses duly recorded. Each person was also asked to describe an ideal candidate as well as one with characteristics that absolutely could not be tolerated on that particular job. The results of these investigations were then formalized into the job descriptions and worker specifications shown. This technique can be applied to a wide variety of plant and office positions.

KEYPUNCH OPERATOR

Job Description

Major Functions
Operates keypunch machine to produce punched tabulating cards, magnetic tapes, and/or diskettes containing numerical and alphabetical information which is the source information to produce machine-readable data.

Type of Supervision
Daily instructions from keypunch leader; general source of supervision is keypunch supervisor.

Equipment Used
Card punch–verify machines, key entry station, program drums, diskettes, diskettes-to-magnetic-tape converters and disk-to-magnetic-tape control unit, and any other input conversion equipment.

Duties
Interprets and analyzes source documents to convert data into cards and/or tapes containing numerical and alphabetical information such as quantities, values, codes, and descriptive information used to produce invoice vouchers, accounts payable vouchers, and statistical information. Captures data from source documents such as freight bills, numerical control sheets, engineering analyses, estimating sheets, sales reports, textile plant production records, personnel records, vacation schedules, and various miscellaneous specified requests. Prepares entry data in accordance with instructions provided by supervisor. Detects errors and reprepares corrected information. Operates equipment to transfer records from disk and diskette storage to tape. Keeps sequence and control of source documents. Rejects source documents that do not contain sufficient information to meet job specification requirements. Performs other clerical duties as directed by supervisor.

KEYPUNCH OPERATOR

Worker Specifications

1. *Required aptitudes:*
   a. High degree of finger dexterity.
   b. High degree of clerical speed and accuracy.

2. *Mental ability:* Average mental capacity. Job requires a limited degree of selection, interpretation, and analysis of materials. Incumbents must use judgment as to the accuracy and validity of source information.

3. *Preemployment training:* Applicant must have been trained to operate a keypunch machine and must have passed the keypunch proficiency test.

4. *Employment training and experience:* It takes the average employee meeting preemployment requirements 7 to 12 months to become proficient on the new job.

5. *Responsibility for performance and materials:* A high degree of attention must be paid to clearly define procedures. Verification of work by others

(continued)

ensures originator's accountability for work. Performance is measured by accuracy and speed.

6. *Responsibility for contacts:* Job requires only routine reporting and exchange of information. It does not require discussion of interpretation or assignments.

7. *Responsibility for the direction of others:* Keypunch operators direct a work force of one other person. They are not responsible for assigning, scheduling, and coordinating the work of others.

8. *Working conditions:* Jobs are located in areas where only moderately disagreeable conditions are present, with moderate noise levels, and few safety hazards.

9. *Other required characteristics:*
   a. Best candidates should be somewhat introverted. There is little or no chitchat during work assignments. Applicants must be able to adapt to a very confining work situation. An extroverted, people-oriented person would be unhappy here.
   b. Must be detail-oriented. Applicant must be able to adjust to a very high degree of detail without becoming excessively bored.

It will be noted from the above worker specifications that a number of the required qualifications can be determined by tests —the necessary mental ability, required aptitudes, and keypunch proficiency. Other characteristics, such as the extent to which the individual is detail-oriented and possesses the required degree of introversion, can be determined through the interview.

MACHINIST

Job Description

Major Functions
Sets up and operates all types of machine tools and performs all types of layout, fitting, and assembly work.

Type of Supervision
Crew leader and production supervisor.

Equipment Used
All types of machine tools such as lathes, shapers, planers, horizontal and vertical boring mills, milling machines; machinist's hand tools and measuring instruments such as wrenches, hammers, scrapers, files, scribes, protractors, micrometers, gauges, levels, squares; various portable power tools such as drills and grinders; blueprints and sketches.

Duties
Receives instructions and prints regarding work assignment. Interprets drawings and sketches; plans and determines working procedure. Performs layout work; makes sketches. Calculates and determines dimen-

(continued)

sions, tapers, indices, and other data, using shop formulas and hand-books. Selects and grinds tools in accordance with the hardness, machina-bility, and other properties of parts or materials to be machined. Procures or makes jigs, fixtures, or machine attachments required for the work to be machined. Sets up and operates all types of machine tools to drill, face, cut, turn, bore, mill, shape, etc., iron, steel, alloys, and nonferrous and nonmetallic materials and parts to precision tolerances and specified finishes, adjusting stops, feeds, and speeds for efficient machining. Checks and measures work with gauges, micrometers, calipers, and other precision measuring instruments. Assembles, fits, aligns, levels, and ad-justs machinery and equipment. Hooks up and directs crane to transfer and position material or parts to be machined or assembled.

MACHINIST

Worker Specifications

1. *Required aptitudes:*
   a. Good numerical ability.
   b. Good spatial visualization.
   c. Good mechanical aptitude.
   d. Good manual dexterity. Manual skills involve using machine and hand tools to perform tasks involving very close tolerances. Manual skills also include setting up and operating many types of different machines.

2. *Mental ability:* Above-average mental ability. Applicant must be able to read blueprints, perform mathematical conversions, calculate tolerances, and plan work within time requirements.

3. *Preemployment training:* The candidate must either be a graduate appren-tice or have accumulated years of on-the-job experience—experience which qualifies him or her to set up and operate a wide variety of machine tools, such as lathes, grinders, drill presses, and milling machines.

4. *Employment training and experience:* It takes the average apprentice graduate 37 to 48 months to become a proficient first-class machinist. Even a skilled, experienced machinist requires 7 to 12 months to adjust to the demands of a new work environment.

5. *Responsibility for performance and materials:* Working with blueprints and materials that require machining to exact tolerances requires a high degree of attention to work being performed. Improperly machined parts have to be remachined or scrapped. Each machinist is responsible for individual work performed. Moderate attention is necessary to avoid damage to ma-chine tools through dropping, improper use, or carelessness.

6. *Responsibility for contacts:* Job requires ordinary courtesy to maintain good working relationships with coworkers. Job requires contact with supervisory personnel in directing assignments to subordinates. Little or no contact with vendors. Telephone communications not required. Interpreta-tion of job assignment *is* required. Exchange of information with other machinists when working on long-range projects is extremely important.

7. *Responsibility for the direction of others:* A machinist directs a normal work

(continued)

force of two or three helpers and one to two laborers. Machinists are responsible for performance of subordinates but do not have disciplinary authority.

8. *Working conditions:* Must be alert to a variety of hazards, such as exposure to cuts, bruises, and possible hand and finger injuries encountered while operating machine tools and handling machine parts. Must be alert to the presence of overhead cranes. Should have some knowledge of other hazards related to working in a shop environment, e.g., slippery floors, noise, and exposure to eye hazards.

9. *Other required characteristics:* Applicants must be willing to wear required eye protection, hard hats, and safety shoes. Ordinary care and attention must be paid to the prevention of injury to others.

The required degree of mental ability and various aptitudes can be determined by means of tests. In many companies, newly hired machinists are given a so-called craft test at the end of 30 days. This is an "on-the-job," i.e., practical, test designed to determine proficiency in setting up and operating a variety of machine tools.

The development of worker specifications is fundamental to the design of a selection program. The remaining steps of the recommended selection program logically follow and are included in the next chapter.

CHAPTER SIX

Selection Procedures

We have previously pointed out that indiscriminate hiring frequently results in the employment of substandard and minimally qualified people and that this, in turn, contributes substantially to high turnover, reduced productivity, excessive employment costs, and even the inability of a given organization to compete effectively in the national and international business arena. Many industries have reached this state of affairs largely because so many personnel people believe that, in today's regulated society, they no longer have the freedom to select the best-qualified employees.

We take the view that it is not only possible but absolutely essential that American industry so revise its current selection procedures that better-qualified employees can be made available. This chapter will introduce a series of recently validated methods for accomplishing this objective.

DESIGN OF A SELECTION PROGRAM

Before discussing the various aspects of an effective selection program, it seems logical to examine some of the preliminary procedures that must be considered prior to the implementation of the program itself. These procedures have much to do with laying the groundwork for future validation of the selection program.

A selection system should be designed in such a way that much of the information can be quantified. For example, to say that prospective employees should have a *good* attendance record on previous jobs is not enough. It is far better to establish an attendance standard for prospective employees based on acceptable attendance standards for present employees. Some companies have a rule that any employee with more than 5 days of unexcused absence within a 3-month period is automatically subject to dismissal. In such a company, then, the same rule should be applied to applicants for employment. Thus, if application information reveals attendance records on previous jobs that do not meet the standards set up in the company for present employees, that applicant should be screened out at the first stage of the selection process.

In setting up physical standards, a system must be established that is fair and applies equally to males and females, and such standards should be flexible, in the sense that they can be altered in order to conform to future needs. For example, if people cannot move up in the organization because of certain environmental or physical factors, it is conceivable that such factors could be changed at some time in the future. Thus, instead of a requirement that involves lifting 50-pound bags, perhaps the product could be shipped in 25-pound bags so that more employees can perform that job. From an efficiency standpoint, it is important to look beyond the short-term effects of a selection procedure to determine the long-term effect of such procedures on the future work force.

A selection system must also have *face validity;* that is, it must be viewed favorably by both applicants and government officials. A system may be totally legal, possessing no adverse impact, but so complicated that it does not make sense or seems to the general public to be unfair. In such a case, the company is asking for trouble.

Postemployment Evaluation and Assistance

Every selection system should provide for postemployment counseling. Interviews with workers after their first few weeks of employment provide interviewers with an important object lesson in terms of how good a job they have done in their initial selection. This often sparks a learning process that results in the tightening of standards and the consideration of factors which were not initially deemed important.

Postemployment counseling can impact importantly upon turnover as well. Unhappy workers can often be provided with information about company policies or long-range promotional possibilities that can change their entire outlook. And in some cases such individuals can be transferred to jobs that make a better utilization of their specific abilities and interests.

The Time Element

Since the number of selection procedures we have already mentioned in passing is greater than those in use in many companies, personnel people may ask themselves, "Where can I find the time to do all of this?" This question becomes all the more meaningful in light of the fact that we are recommending an employment interview which in itself will require 35 to 45 minutes of the interviewer's time.

If an employment office has historically accepted 1200 to 1500 applications a year and hired 300 people, the chances are that all 1200 to 1500 people have been given a 10- to 15-minute interview, with that interview being pretty much the sole basis for selection or rejection. It is small wonder, then, that personnel people worry about the time element in a selection system that includes a 35- to 45-minute employment interview. Some may even say to themselves, "I am certainly going to have to hire more interviewers if I adopt this system." *In actual operation, however, this need not be the case at all.* We have used an inverted pyramid (Figure 1) to demonstrate that applicants can be screened out at all stages of the selection program, in such a way that only a fraction of the initial population survive to the point of meriting an employment interview. Thus, as many as 50 percent of the initial population may often be screened out on the basis of the application form and preliminary interview, with 20 to 25 percent

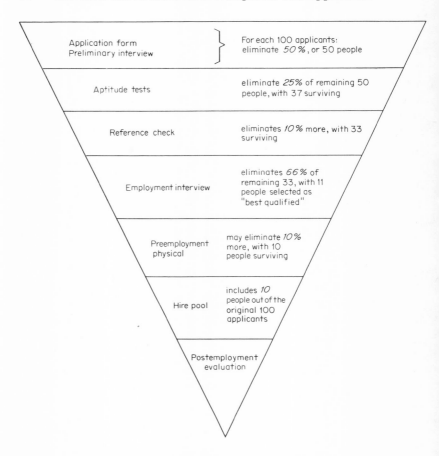

FIG. 1   Inverted pyramid of selection.

of the remainder screened out on the basis of inability to pass the employment tests. Of those remaining, 10 percent may be eliminated following reference checks. This means that, out of a population of 1500 applicants a year for various jobs, employment interviews may need to be carried out on as few as 500 people. This number spread out over a period of a year certainly does not represent a very heavy load. Specific numbers of people screened out at various stages of the selection system will vary, depending on the quality of the applicants. But such variations generally balance out when large numbers of applicants are screened through the system. Figure 1 demonstrates that, given a sufficient number of applicants for a specific job, or looking at a large number of applicants for a composite of many jobs, only about 10 of every 100 applicants survive as "best-qualified."

Those best-qualified candidates for whom jobs may not be immediately available are placed in an active file and are contacted wherever they may be when new job openings occur. It is far less costly to "track down" good people who have already been processed than to move new applicants through the entire selection procedure. If all the best-qualified applicants are ultimately hired, the company is using a selection ratio of 10 applicants for every person hired.

The State Employment Service

It will probably come as a surprise to many companies that the state employment service stands ready to do much of the prescreening job. This agency will screen applicants to company specifications and even administer a variety of employment tests that have already been validated for large assortments of jobs. Utilization of state employment services represents a terrific boon to many organizations since they can get the benefits of test results without having to worry about whether or not such results will stand up to the scrutiny of federal investigators. State employment services have at their disposal tests developed and validated by the United States Employment Service (USES). These tests are available with appropriate norms. It should be apparent that a service such as this provided by the state enables an employer to concentrate on lower steps of the selection pyramid. In the event that the state employment service does the prescreening, though, it seems likely that an organization may wish to increase its selection ratio, at the employment interview level, from perhaps two or three to one up to four to one. This is another way of saying that company employment interviewers would expect to interview as many as four persons in order to select one, rather than the two or three persons who would normally be interviewed if all of the prescreening were done by the company itself.

Because of a decrease in available funds, some states may no longer be able to provide industry with prescreening employment services. In that event, companies may be able to use computerized systems to screen applicants on the basis of application form information.

When state employment services assistance is requested, this request must be put in writing. And it must be agreed in the request that actions taken by the state on behalf of an employer are the liability of the employer, not of the state. It is, therefore, very much to the employer's advantage to know exactly what the state is doing so that the employer can, if necessary, defend this procedure.

Having discussed the design of a selection program, it is now time to take a closer look at the selection procedures themselves. It must be pointed out at the outset, however, that it is not the purpose of this book to present selection procedures that can be adapted to every specific plant and office situation. Nor do the authors make any guarantee that adoption of the suggested procedures will automatically enable a company to avoid legal difficulties. For, after all, it is *how* the procedures are used and how appropriate they are for any given situation that determine overall effectiveness. If a company does not have a staff well-versed in the intricacies of today's employment situation, it would be well-advised to secure the services of a knowledgeable consultant.

In this chapter we are primarily concerned with the establishment of a selection framework that can be used as a base upon which any given organization can build a program suitable to its individual needs. Hence, our emphasis is upon *concepts* of selection procedures and examples of *some* of the things that can be done.

THE APPLICATION FORM

It is probably not too strong a statement that a vast majority of companies in this country have application forms that are woefully inadequate and that some are actually illegal. Most of us know by this time that it is no longer legal to ask an applicant's specific age, marital status, or number of dependents, yet a surprising number of applications currently in use still require some of this information.

Our biggest quarrel with most application forms, though, involves errors of omission, rather than commission. They simply do not require enough information. Since as much as 50 percent of the original applicant population can be screened out on the basis of information contained on the application form, it seems only logical that this form contain as much information as possible. Remember, too, that the elimination of a sizable number of applicants at this first stage of the selection process can save the personnel department a great deal of time and money. (See the suggested application form on pages 82 to 84.)

The employment application form shown here would of course have to be modified to fit the specific needs of an individual company. Obviously, too, the form should provide space for coded information with respect to sex and race. Only in this way can the employment office monitor the applicant flow and ensure the selection of a sufficient number of minorities and females to meet its affirmative action goals.

Reference to the application form will reveal that it is possible to design a form suitable for all entry-level positions—in the office as well as the plant.

The Application Form as a Basis for Eliminating Applicants

In Chapter 5 it was noted that worker specifications represent the base upon which all selection procedures are built. For jobs for which the specifications indicate a minimum number of years of specific experience or education, therefore, application forms can be quickly scanned to determine whether or not the individual fulfills those requirements. Those applicants who do not have sufficient experience or education can be screened out at this time.

If, in the interest of hiring people with good job stability, the company has a requirement in writing that it will not hire individuals with more than two jobs during the past 5 years, additional candidates can be eliminated on that basis.

Gaps in dates of employment—except in the case of full-time homemakers—represent a source of further concern. If such gaps cannot be satisfactorily explained in the subsequent preliminary interview, some individuals may be eliminated on this basis.

Since most companies are looking for people who are promotable, failure to move ahead or to achieve reasonable raises in pay over a period of time raises further questions—questions that must be discussed in the preliminary interview.

If a job under consideration requires a fair degree of mathematical facility, persons who least liked "number crunching" on previous jobs and least liked mathematics in high school or college might be regarded in a less favorable light. If all other aspects of the individual's history seem suitable, however, such a person

Date_____

XYZ COMPANY

Employment Application Form

Complete application form carefully and truthfully because this company uses this form to screen candidates for jobs and because your information may be checked with previous employers and schools.

Type of work desired	First choice	Second choice

Personal Data

Last name (print) First Middle	Social Security number

Address (no., street, city, state) Zip code	Telephone number Area code ( )

Have you worked for XYZ before? ☐ Yes ☐ No	Where?	When?

Have you applied here before? ☐ Yes ☐ No	When?

Are you a U.S. citizen? ☐ Yes ☐ No	If no, enter alien registration number

Age (check one)   ☐ Under 18   ☐ 18–20   ☐ 21–69   ☐ Over 69

Are you willing to work shifts? ☐ Yes ☐ No	Are you willing to work weekends? ☐ Yes ☐ No

Are you available to work   ☐ full-time?   ☐ part-time?

Outside interests—(clubs, hobbies, sports, community activities, etc.)

Work Experience

Last job (or present position)	Name and address of employer

Date started _____   Date left _____

Beginning job _____   Beginning pay _____ per hour/per week

Final job _____   Final pay _____ per hour/per week

(continued)

Description of duties on final job

What did you like best about the job?

What did you like least about the job?

Reasons for leaving

Second last job	Name and address of employer

Date started _____ Date left _____

Beginning job _____ Beginning pay _____ per hour/per week

Final job _____ Final pay _____ per hour/per week

Description of duties on final job

What did you like best about the job?

What did you like least about the job?

Reason(s) for leaving

Third last job	Name and address of employer

Date started _____ Date left _____

Beginning job _____ Beginning pay _____ per hour/per week

Final job _____ Final pay _____ per hour/per week

Description of duties on final job

(continued)

What did you like best about the job?

What did you like least about the job?

Reason(s) for leaving

Education

	Name of school	City and state	Highest grade completed	Diploma or degree
Grade school				
High school				
Trade school				
Business school				
College				
Best-liked subjects				
Least-liked subjects				

Were your grades generally ☐average? ☐above average? ☐below average?

In the event of employment, I understand that false or misleading information given in my application or interview(s) may result in discharge. I understand, also, that I am required to abide by all rules and regulations of the company.

_____   _____
Signature of applicant   Date

might be passed on to the employment test stage in an effort to determine just how much mathematical aptitude the person possesses.

If the job requires shift work and if the applicant indicates distaste for shift work or flat refusal to do it, elimination becomes automatic.

THE PRELIMINARY INTERVIEW

Although preliminary interviews can usually be completed in a period of 3 to 5 minutes, they nevertheless occupy a place of importance in the selection process. In smaller organizations, the preliminary interview will probably be carried out immediately after the applicant has completed the application form. One of the main purposes of this interview is to make sure that the candidate has responded to all questions on the application form.

In some larger firms candidates are invited to return for their preliminary interview on some subsequent day. Such firms believe that a willingness to return for further evaluation on another day provides one measure of a candidate's interest in going to work for that company. In any event, there should be someone from personnel on hand to check application forms for accuracy and completeness before the individual is allowed to leave the premises.

The Application as a Guide
to the Preliminary Interview

Preliminary interviewers usually use the completed application as a basis for their brief discussion with applicants. As indicated in the previous section, they raise such questions as (1) relevancy and adequacy of experience and education, (2) gaps in employment dates, (3) willingness to work shifts and weekends, and (4) specific type of job desired.

It should be pointed out here, however, that only those candidates who are obviously unqualified should be screened out by means of the application and preliminary interview. Doubtful cases should be screened in, thus giving the individual an opportunity to take the employment test and perhaps to participate in the final employment interview.

Preliminary interviewers with appropriate experience and

training can frequently bring to light information that should be followed up in the final interview, and, of course, they should document such information if possible. For example, the interviewer may be dissatisfied with the candidate's reasons for leaving her or his last job, even though general impressions of the applicant are otherwise favorable, or the interviewer may get the feeling that an applicant is not telling the truth but, lacking sufficient time, may not be able to document this sufficiently. In both cases these impressions should be passed on for further elucidation, together with any documentation supporting them.

Obtaining Candidates' Permission for Reference Checks

Candidates for employment should be asked to authorize their prospective employer to carry out reference checks on previous places of employment, *whether or not the company plans to make such a check on every applicant.* Studies have shown that there is often an appreciable difference between information provided on an application form and information provided by previous employers. This means, of course, that some applicants tend to exaggerate and some applicants fail to tell the truth. But if applicants have signed a statement authorizing a prospective employer to verify application information, they are more likely to tell the truth, particularly since such statements usually include a clause that any misrepresentation will be cause for elimination from employment consideration or for immediate discharge. Having signed such a statement, moreover, individuals are more likely during the final interview to provide a truthful account of their vocational and educational history.

Preliminary interviewers should carefully observe applicants' behavior at the time they sign the authorization for release of information. If they seem at all reluctant or tentative, this observation should be recorded and passed along to the person who carries out the final interview.

Applicants who are not screened out on the basis of the application form and the preliminary interview should be told about the next step in the selection program—employment tests. Whenever possible, employment tests should be given on the same day that the preliminary interview takes place.

EMPLOYMENT TESTS

Aptitude tests have a long history of reliability in measuring aptitudes in the plant and office setting. In fact, aptitude tests represent a far more accurate tool for measuring certain ability factors than does any other known device. Thus, tests of mental ability, verbal ability, numerical ability, mechanical comprehension, clerical aptitude, and manual dexterity provide more valid results than can be obtained by means of the interview, no matter how well-trained the interviewer may be. It therefore seems most unfortunate that so many companies have eliminated testing from their selection programs. Such companies have mistakenly and needlessly eliminated testing because they believe this is no longer possible under EEO regulations. Nothing could be further from the truth. EEO regulations simply require that there be a positive relationship between the test and performance on the job. If such a relationship cannot be demonstrated, the test should not be in use anyway since it yields no helpful selection information.

The development and validation of employment tests for a specific plant or office situation, however, require an expertise which the personnel departments of most companies do not have. If they want to develop their own tests, therefore, companies would be well-advised to enlist the services of a competent consultant.

Transportability

Transportability, or validity generalization, as some refer to it, is a magic characteristic that makes possible a much wider utilization of aptitude tests than is generally known. The term simply means that if a test can be shown to be valid for a given job in one plant situation, that same test can be assumed to be valid *for that specific job* in other plant locations. In a class action suit (*Pegues v. Mississippi State Employment Service*[1]) in the U.S. District Court for the Northern District of Mississippi, the court stated: "Allegation that validity is specific to a particular location, a particular set of tasks, and to a specific applicant population is not true." In support of this opinion, it has further been stated (*Friend and Fuller et al. v. Leidinger, Fulton, Thorton, and Fionegan*), in the U.S. Court of Appeals for the Fourth District: "To require local

---

[1] 488 F. Supp. 239 (D. Miss. 1980).

validation in every city, village, and hamlet would be ludicrous." These rulings, then, enable an organization to use tests *that have already been validated elsewhere* for certain specific jobs, or if a corporation has developed and validated a test for a given job in one plant or office setup, the rulings enable it to use this same test in the selection of applicants for the same job in its other plants and offices.

The Psychological Corporation's General Clerical Test

Some years ago the Psychological Corporation (now part of the publishing house Harcourt, Brace, Jovanavich at 757 Third Avenue, New York City) developed and validated an excellent test of clerical aptitude. This test provides three subscores—clerical (checking, alphabetizing, and error location), numerical (arithmetic computation and arithmetic reasoning), and verbal (spelling, reading comprehension, vocabulary, and grammar). The test is in wide use today and is a valuable selection tool in the employment of clerical people, particularly for higher-level clerical positions.

U.S. Employment Service

For those companies that do not wish to take the time or incur the expense of developing their own employment tests, there is an alternative. The U.S. Employment Service (USES) of the U.S. Department of Labor has developed a General Aptitude Test Battery (GATB) which has been in use since 1947 by state employment service offices. Since that time, the GATB has been one of a number of tests included in a continuing program of research for the purpose of validating tests against success in many different occupations. For some strange reason, the existence of GATB is not widely known or understood in industry. Yet, as indicated earlier in this chapter, any company, large or small, can ask its state employment service to administer appropriate tests as an important part of its selection procedures.

The GATB is made up of nine specific tests. They are as follows: general learning ability (vocabulary and arithmetic reasoning), verbal aptitude (vocabulary), numerical aptitude (computation and arithmetic reasoning), spatial aptitude (three-dimensional space perception), form perception (tool matching and form matching), clerical perception (name comparison), motor coordination (mark making), finger dexterity (assembly and disassembly), and manual dexterity (placing and turning). The manual for the GATB describes the nine different tests as follows:

G *(general learning ability)* Ability to catch on or understand instructions and underlying principles; ability to reason and make judgments. Closely related to doing well in school.

V *(verbal aptitude)* Ability to understand the meaning of words and to use them effectively; ability to comprehend language, to understand relationships between words, and to understand the meanings of whole sentences and paragraphs.

N *(numerical aptitude)* Ability to perform arithmetic operations quickly and accurately.

S *(spatial aptitude)* Ability to think visually of geometric forms and to comprehend two-dimensional representations of three-dimensional objects; ability to recognize relationships resulting from the movements of objects in space.

P *(form perception)* Ability to perceive pertinent details in objects or in pictorial or graph material; ability to make a visual comparison and discrimination and see slight differences in shapes and shadings of figures and widths and lengths of lines.

Q *(clerical perception)* Ability to perceive pertinent details in verbal or tabular material; ability to observe differences in copy, to proofread words and numbers, and to avoid perceptual errors in arithmetic computation. A measure of speed of perception which is required in many industrial jobs even when the job does not have verbal or numerical content.

K *(motor coordination)* Ability to coordinate eyes with hands or fingers rapidly and accurately and to make precise movements with speed; ability to make a movement response accurately and swiftly.

F *(finger dexterity)* Ability to move the fingers and manipulate small objects with the fingers, rapidly or accurately.

M *(manual dexterity)* Ability to move the hands easily and skillfully; ability to work with the hands in placing and turning motions.

Over the years, USES has developed and validated tests on an astonishing number of plant and office jobs. Of course, norms have been developed for each test which make it possible to determine how well a given applicant scores in comparison with the population upon which the test was standardized. Thus, one individual may obtain a score superior to the scores of 90 percent of the population upon which the test was standardized; another individual's score may be superior to those of only 25 percent of that population, the lowest quarter. Test norms for specific occupations also provide *minimum aptitude scores,* the score below which the individual is not likely to be successful on that job.

Obviously, an applicant for any given job would *not* be expected to take all nine tests. As a matter of fact, most jobs involve only three or four tests. A machinist, for example, would only be required to take tests N (numerical aptitude), S (spatial aptitude), and M (manual dexterity). An employment clerk, on the other hand, would be required to take G (general learning ability), V (verbal aptitude), N (numerical aptitude), and Q (clerical perception).

Because the GATB was developed by the federal government, it is available in *all* the various state employment offices. In order to take advantage of this testing service, a company need only contact its state employment service. The state will administer the appropriate tests for the specific job involved.

The best part of all of this is that all the tests have already been validated and, because of the concept of transportability, they can be utilized in any plant or office situation, *so long as the job for which the applicant is being tested is the same as the job upon which the test has been standardized.* This means that the test results can be used without fear of criticism by government inspectors.

Since most people have very little conception of the vast array of jobs for which tests have been validated by the USES, such positions most frequently found in plant and office are listed on pages 91 to 94. This information is taken from the *Manual for the USES General Aptitude Test Battery, 1980.*

The validity and professionalism of aptitude tests administered by the nationwide network of 2500 public employment service (job service) offices were supported by a recent federal court decision which struck down allegations of unlawful discrimination against minorities and women.

In a decision in a class action suit referred to earlier in this chapter (*Pegues v. Mississippi State Employment Service*[2]), Feder-

---

[2] 488 F. Supp. 239 (D. Miss. 1980).

Asbestos Products
Braiding machine operator
Loom fixer
Spinner, frame
Twister tender
Weaver

Automobiles
Assembler, automobile
Assembler, trailer

Automotive Services
Automobile body repairer
Automobile mechanic
Painter, transportation
equipment

Bakery Products
Baker
Bakery worker

Boilers
Boilermaker I

Boots and Shoes
Hand sewer, shoes
Stitcher, standard machine

*Brick, Tile, and Nonclay
Refractories*
Paster
Tile sorter

Building Board
Fourdrinier machine tender

Canning and Preserving
Cannery worker
Laborer, shellfish processing
Sorter, agricultural produce

Carpets and Rugs
Burler
Construction-equipment
mechanic
Construction worker I
Floor layer
Glazier
Lather
Operating engineer
Ornamental iron worker
Painter
Pipe fitter
Plasterer
Plumber
Roofer
Structural steel worker
Taper

Electrical Equipment
Appliance assembler, line
Assembler and wirer,
industrial equipment
Assembler, dry cell and
battery
Assembler, electrical
accessories I
Cable maker
Coil winder
Electric motor assembler
Firesetter
Light bulb assembler
Plug wirer

Electronics
Cable maker
Coil winder
Electronics assembler
Firesetter
Supervisor, electronics
Tube assembler, electron

Engines and Turbines
Assembler, internal-
combustion engine
Machinery erector

Fabricated Plastics
Blow-molding machine
operator
Compression-molding
machine tender
Extruder operator
Finisher, hand
Injection-molding machine
tender

Financial Institutions
Credit analyst
Proof machine operator
Teller

*Food Preparations and Food
Specialties (Not Classified
Elsewhere)*
Quality control technician

Foundry
Die-casting machine
operator II
Foundry worker, general
Molder
Patternmaker, metal
Patternmaker, wood
Sand slinger operator

Furniture
Assembler, metal furniture
Upholsterer, inside
Glass Manufacturing
Forming machine operator
Selector
Twister tender
Glass Products
Glass blower, laboratory
apparatus
Gloves and Mittens
Glove sewer
Hats and Caps
Hat and cap sewer
Heat Treating
Heat treater I
Heat treater II
Hosiery
Boarding machine operator
Knitting machine fixer
Looper
Pairer
Seamless hosiery knitter
Sewing machine operator
Stocking inspector
Instruments and Apparatus
Assembler
Assembler, hospital supplies
Glass blower, laboratory
apparatus
Inspector, mechanical and
electrical
Insulated Wire and Cable
Extruding machine operator
Insulating machine operator
Pairing machine operator
Insurance
Claims adjuster
Underwriter
Iron and Steel
Cold mill operator
Guide setter
Inspector
Labor, general
Manipulator
Screw-down operator
Second helper
Tube drawer
Jewelry
Ring maker

Knit Goods
Knitting machine fixer
Knitting machine operator
Looper
Warp-knitting machine
operator
Laundry
Assembler
Flatwork finisher
Linen supply load builder
Lighting Fixtures
Assembler I
Machinery Manufacturing
Assembler and wirer,
industrial equipment
Machinery erector
Manufacturer's service
representative
Machine Shop
Cutoff saw operator, metal
Machinist
Production machine tender
Screw machine setup operator,
production
Tool and die maker
Turret lathe setup
operator, tool
Machine Tools and Accessories
Manufacturer's service
representative
Manufactured Buildings
Taper
Narrow Fabrics
Braiding machine operator
Loom fixer
*Nonferrous Metal Alloys and
Primary Products*
Rolling mill operator
Tube drawer
Optical Goods
Precision lens grinder
*Ordnance and Accessories (Not
Classified Elsewhere)*
Process inspector
Paper and Pulp
Back tender, paper machine
Fourdrinier machine tender
Log scaler
Paper sorter and counter

Paper Goods
  Bag machine operator
  Cylinder die machine operator
  Die maker
  Envelope-folding machine
    adjuster
  Flexographic press operator
  Folding machine operator
  Machine setup operator,
    paper goods
  Printer-slotter operator
  Rewinder operator
  Scrapper
*Petroleum and Natural Gas
Production*
  Drafter, geological
  Rotary driller helper
Petroleum Refining
  Refinery operator
  Tank truck driver
Phonograph Products
  Injection-molding machine
    tender
  Record press tender
Photofinishing
  Mounter, automatic
  Photograph finisher
  Printer operator,
    black and white
Plastics Materials
  Extruder operator
Pottery and Porcelain Ware
  Inspector
  Kiln placer
Printing and Publishing
  Bindery worker
  Flexographic press
    operator
  Folding machine operator
  Lithographic plate maker
  Mailing machine operator
  Manager, circulation
  Offset press operator I
  Photographer, lithographic
  Process artist
  Proofreader
  Stripper
  Web press operator
*Refrigerators and Refrigerating
and Ice-Making Equipment*
  Appliance assembler, line

Retail Trade
  Carpet layer
  Cashier-checker
  Driver, sales route
  Floor layer
  Manager, automobile
    service station
  Manager, department
  Manager, retail store
  Meat cutter
  Sales clerk
  Salesperson, general
    merchandise
  Tank trunk driver
  Venetian blind assembler
Rubber Goods
  Injection-molding machine
    tender
  Press tender
  Rubber goods inspector-tester
  V-belt coverer
Rubber Reclaiming
  Rubber goods inspector-tester
Rubber Tires and Tubes
  Press tender
  Rubber goods inspector-tester
  Tire builder, automobile
*Ship and Boat Building and
Repairing*
  Shipfitter
Slaughtering and Meat-Packing
  Poultry dressing worker
Synthetic Fibers
  Twister tender
  Yarn-texturing machine
    operator
Telephone and Telegraph
  Central office operator
  Central office repairer
Textiles
  Balling machine operator
  Burler
  Covering machine operator
  Loom fixer
  Mender
  Spinner, frame
  Spooler operator,
    automatic
  Twister tender
  Weaver

Textile Products (Not Classified Elsewhere)
Levers lace machine operator

Tobacco Products
Cigarette inspector
Stemmer, machine

Toys, Games, and Playground Equipment
Finisher, hand
Toy assembler

Trimmings and Embroidery, Stitching, and Pleating
Carding machine operator

Waterworks
Water treatment plant operator

Welding and Related Processes
Machine feeder

Solderer, production line
Thermal cutter, hand, I
Welder, arc
Welder, combination
Welder, production line

Wholesale Trade
Driver, sales route
Meat cutter
Packer, agricultural produce
Salesperson, general merchandise
Sales representative, construction machinery
Sorter, agricultural produce
Tank truck driver

Woodworking
Cabinetmaker
Machinist, wood

al Judge Orma R. Smith found no evidence of discrimination by either the Mississippi State Employment Service (MSES) or USES through use of USES aptitude tests. Judge Smith also found no evidence of adverse impact on women or minorities. The aptitude tests for table work, licensed practical nurse, and nurse aide were at issue in the case.

Judge Smith ruled that the procedures for validation and standardization for USES tests are nondiscriminatory and conform to professional standards and EEOC guidelines on employee selection procedures. The judge said: "The SATBs [Specific Aptitude Test Battery] used by the Cleveland [Miss.] job service office were properly validated and did not unlawfully discriminate against minorities." The SATB is used as a measure of potential for success in a specific occupation, rather than as a general aptitude test. The decision is being appealed.

Test Results as an Aid to the Final Interviewer

Test results can often provide an interviewer clues to the individual's motivation. Let us take the example of a woman whose general learning ability is very high. This means, of course, that she is potentially capable of outstanding academic performance. If, in the final interview, this individual admits her grades in school were mediocre, it becomes apparent to the interviewer that she may not have applied herself in school and may thus have a tendency to be lazy. On the other hand, another female applicant with a mediocre general learning ability score who claims to have made outstanding grades in school either is lying or, if she is telling the truth, must have worked so hard to get those grades that she has developed great application, perseverance, and self-discipline. The latter finding would indicate the so-called overachiever, one who manages to surpass the level denoted by his or her basic ability. Having discovered that he or she is appraising an overachiever, the interviewer would naturally want to know what prompted the applicant's needs in this direction. Subsequent findings might conceivably play an important part in understanding the individual's basic personality structure.

Limitations of Tests

Despite the space given to the discussion of employment tests in this chapter, we do not wish to give the impression that tests alone can be expected to do the entire selection job. To understand this, one only has to refer again to worker specifications for most plant and office jobs. Among other things, such specifications will normally list factors such as willingness to work, ability to get along with other people, emotional maturity, and ability to take pressure —none of which factors can be measured accurately by tests. Fortunately, however, a well-trained interviewer can pick up where the tests leave off, evaluating such factors. This is why a large portion of this book is devoted to the final interview.

THE REFERENCE CHECK

Those applicants who have survived screening by application, preliminary interview, and employment tests are now ready for the reference check and the final interview. Although it would be preferable to check the references of applicants before the final interview, in most cases it is not practical to wait for the return of the reference check information before proceeding with the final interview. Hence, it is better to complete the final interview and then run reference checks on only those who have survived that final stage of the selection process.

Reference checks have their limitations, primarily because some previous employers fail to respond and those who do respond are often reluctant to record any negative information. For the latter reason, it is best to request only factual information such as dates of employment, positions held, reasons for leaving, and attendance record (see the sample reference check form on page 97).

As a matter of practicality, reference checks are usually run on only the last 5 years of employment, and it is only sensible to ask about attendance records over the past 2 years.

In today's world, it is important that reference checks be carried out by mail only. In large corporations, it may not be possible to run a check on every single person to be hired. In that case, the company will check one out of three or perhaps one out of five, making certain that on a percentage basis it processes an equal percentage of white males, females, and minority applicants.

Where Discrepancies Occur

In those situations where information of a derogatory nature is returned to the company by a previous employer or where there is a serious discrepancy with information contained on the application form, the applicant must be given an opportunity to present his or her side of the story. If the discrepancy is sufficiently serious and if the applicant fails to convince the interviewer of his or her honesty, the applicant is normally turned down for employment. If that person is already employed, he or she will usually be terminated. In all fairness, though, such an applicant must be given a hearing.

THE FINAL INTERVIEW

Since a major portion of this book is devoted to the final interview, only passing reference to that important selection procedure will be made at this point. Suffice it to say here that, in the hands of an experienced, well-trained interviewer, this final aspect of the selection program is the most important of all. It is here that all information from previous selection steps is integrated and the final hiring decision made.

PHYSICAL EXAMINATION

Since the physical examination may cost the company anywhere from $50 to $100 per person, only those who survive the final

XYZ COMPANY

Reference Check   Date _____

Applicant's name _____

Applicant's Social Security number _____

Dear Sir or Madam:

We would be most appreciative if you would supply information on the above-named individual who has named you as a previous employer.

Dates of employment	Positions held
From _____	
To _____	

Reasons for termination

Attendance record (days absent during the last 12 months of employment)	Signature and title
	_____
	_____

Your cooperation in this matter will be reciprocated. Thank you very much.

Sincerely yours,

Authorization for Release of Information

Please be advised that I authorize XYZ Company to exercise the right, now or in the future, to verify the information I have provided them, and I authorize my previous employers and schools to release the information requested to XYZ. I understand that any misrepresentation will be cause for elimination from employment consideration or for immediate discharge.

_____   _____
Signature   Date

interview are referred to the medical department. The principal purpose of the physical examination is to determine if applicants can physically perform the work for which they are being hired. This is a decision that only a qualified physician can make and, hence, should never be made by anyone in the personnel department.

Documentation

In this area as well as in all the other selection steps, a record must be compiled as to why the individual was medically rejected or limited for employment. The notation may be brief, but it must be specific and to the point. This applies to individuals screened out earlier in the selection process as well—at the application form stage, the preliminary interview stage, the employment test stage, and the final interview stage. Medical documentation should be done by a medical department representative and not by the interviewer. All comments should be dated and signed for future verification.

OTHER EMPLOYMENT CONSIDERATIONS

Some personnel people mistakenly believe that their responsibility ends once the applicant has been hired and placed on a job. This attitude is shortsighted and reflects lack of understanding of the complete personnel function. As indicated earlier, interviewers should make a practice of scheduling postemployment discussions with people they have employed. For one thing, this provides an opportunity to evaluate their initial judgment in the hiring situation. When this judgment seems to have been in error, interviewers learn from their mistakes. They sometimes realize that they need to tighten their selection standards or to be more careful in their placement of individuals in terms of the kind of a job that makes best use of their ability. There is a further bonus that may result from postemployment interviews—that of effecting job transfers before it is too late. In certain cases, it becomes obvious that an employee who is unhappy and perhaps not particularly well-qualified in his or her present position could be expected to do far better in another type of job. In putting into effect such a transfer, interviewers often "save" an employee who might otherwise have become a turnover statistic.

Maintain the Same Standards
for All Applicants

Once the organization has set up hiring standards—whether they involve test results or interview findings—those standards should be maintained for *all* applicants. In their efforts to hire a greater number of minorities in a hurry, for example, some companies employ people with lower test results or hire individuals who did not quite meet final interview hiring standards. This is a serious mistake, for it means that people are being employed who will not be competitive in the work situation. Such individuals join the company on an unequal footing with their better-qualified peers, and this not only makes it difficult for them to perform their initial job satisfactorily but also makes it *almost impossible for them to progress to higher-level responsibilities*. Therefore, it makes more sense to stick to the same standards for all employees, even if it means the expenditure of more effort and money on the recruiting function. Recent research supports this view:

> Seven or eight years ago, GE decided to get the government off its back by dropping all tests of job aptitude, and "getting their numbers right" in the hiring process. Like many firms, GE has a policy of hiring from within. About a year ago, several plants realized that a large percentage of the people hired under the new selection standards were not promotable. GE had merely transferred the adverse impact from the hiring stage to the promotion stage. These plants have now resumed testing (although they are having an outside organization do the testing).[3]

Monitor Adverse Impact

If the overall selection rate for any racial, ethnic, or sex group is less than 80 percent of that of the most successful group (typically whites or males), this will generally be deemed prima facie, i.e., initial, evidence of discrimination because the selection process has *adverse impact* on that group. The key word in the above statement is the word "rate." Thus, if 100 men applied for jobs in a given month and 20 were hired, the *rate of hire* would be 20 percent. If 50 women applied for work and 10 were hired, the rate of hire again would be 20 percent, or equal to the rate at which

---

[3] Frank L. Schmidt and John E. Hunter, "New Research Findings in Personnel Selection: Myths Meet Realities in the '80's," in *Public Personnel Administration—Policies and Practices for Personnel Service*, Prentice-Hall, Englewood Cliffs, N.J., 1981.

men were being hired. If the number of women hired during that month dropped to eight, the company would still be in a reasonably good EEO posture because those eight women would represent 80 percent of the *rate* at which the men were hired. In the event that the number of women hired dropped below eight, however, the selection procedure in use could be said to have adverse impact on women.

The example cited above underlines the importance of monitoring the applicant flow on a monthly basis. Thus, if the employment of females and minorities in a given month reflects a rate of less than 80 percent of the rate at which white males were employed, the company must make up for this deficiency in the succeeding month in order to avoid adverse impact.

If the bottom line of the selection program reflects adverse impact on a specific group, government inspectors may insist that each component procedure of the overall selection process be examined for adverse impact on the group in question, using the same 80 percent rule. (See Figure 2 for an explanation of "bottom line.") Components generally need not be examined if the overall process does not have adverse impact. The employer has four choices to forestall the liability of components having adverse impact:

1. Demonstrate the job-relatedness of the selection procedure.

2. Modify the procedure so that the adverse impact is eliminated, or modify the method of use of the selection procedure to eliminate adverse impact.

3. Terminate the procedure and adopt a different procedure that does not produce adverse impact.

4. Justify the procedure in question to show business necessity for continuing to use it.

If an employer chooses to take step 1 indicated above—that of demonstrating the job-relatedness of the selection procedure—EEO guidelines then require the employer to conduct a detailed and technical validation study, to keep detailed records, and to investigate alternatives that may have less adverse impact. It is therefore abundantly clear that it is very much to any company's advantage to monitor its selection procedure for the purpose of avoiding adverse impact. Experience has shown that it is very

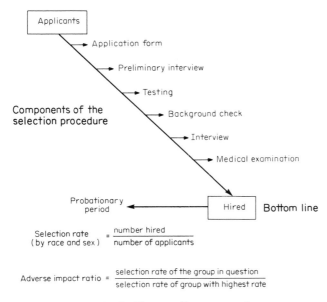

FIG. 2 Bottom-line concept.

difficult to defend adverse impact on minorities or females. It is not only very difficult but also very costly. The word must go out, therefore, to watch the *bottom line*. When periodic analyses— done at least quarterly—indicate that the bottom line reflects no adverse impact, it is possible to be more flexible about the various selection components.

Validation

The term "validation" is often confusing and even a little frightening to personnel people without statistical training. In essence, however, it is simply an attempt to determine whether or not the selection program is producing positive results. The major problem in any validation study is determining an appropriate *criterion*—a measure or standard against which the selection program can be judged or evaluated. So often *supervisors' ratings* represent the only practical criterion that can be found. Yet, such ratings are often replete with errors and inconsistencies. A supervisor whose standards are high tends to rate subordinates harshly, giving them lower ratings than they perhaps deserve. On the other hand, a supervisor whose personal standards are relatively low tends to rate subordinates too leniently, giving them higher ratings than they perhaps deserve. Even so, supervisory ratings frequently represent an acceptable criterion. Far better criteria, though, are those which are based upon *factual evidence*, such as salary increases over a period of some years or rate of turnover.

Since the selection of hourly workers in a great many companies tends to be haphazard or even indiscriminate, it should not be difficult to show a positive relationship between the results of a selection program such as the one detailed in this book and almost any reasonable criterion. A comparison of the rate of turnover among employees hired under this recommended selection program versus the turnover rate *before* the program was inaugurated certainly should show a very positive trend. In the event that a company has maintained a record of supervisory ratings over a period of time, this too should make an interesting and valid study —the comparison of ratings obtained by employees before and after the inauguration of the new selection program. If a program has any merit, it should produce employees with fewer low ratings and more high ratings.

Although the pressure of government regulations probably represents the main force behind a great many validation studies, this should not be the case. Any company inaugurating a new program—particularly a program that involves a fair amount of expense—should be interested in whether or not it works. Why go to all the trouble of developing and installing a new program if effectiveness is simply *assumed* rather than statistically verified? Validation, or *evaluation,* as many personnel people like to call it, should occupy a place at the very heart of a modern personnel operation. Those with responsibility for running the department should be interested in the effectiveness of everything that is done, so that modifications and improvements can be made.

A final point should be made about validation. It is much easier to validate the effectiveness of the overall program than it is to validate any of the individual selection procedures. This is understandable since each procedure is only *part of the whole* and hence could not be expected to show as positive a relationship as the effectiveness of the total program. This is one reason why we have put so much emphasis on the bottom-line concept. If the bottom line, or end result of the entire program, shows no adverse impact, government inspectors are not likely to insist upon the validation of each and every selection procedure that makes up the entire program.

How to Handle the Rejected Applicant

Even though preliminary interviewers or final interviewers make an immediate decision concerning applicants who should not be hired, this information should not be imparted to applicants at the time of the interview. Rather, they should be told that their qualifications as reflected on their application form, test results, and final interview will be compared with those of other applicants applying for the same job. They then should be told that they will subsequently be notified in the event that their qualifications compare favorably with those of other applicants. This approach gives individuals the feeling that their overall qualifications are being given additional consideration and hence does not undermine their sense of self-worth to the extent that a flat "no" might do at the end of an interview.

In the event that an applicant returns to the employment office with a request as to why he or she was not hired, that person should simply be told that there were other applicants whose work experience and education were more suitable for the job in question. This is a statement that most persons can accept, particularly since they do not know who the other applicants are. It is a mistake of major proportions, on the other hand, to tell applicants that they were rejected because they were lacking in certain personality qualifications or because they did not do well enough in the tests. Comments such as these are hard to take and needlessly undermine the individuals' self-confidence.

ILLUSTRATION OF AN ACTUAL SELECTION PROCEDURE

The sample employee selection procedure on pages 105 to 109 encompasses all the selection steps discussed in this chapter. It meets all the legal selection requirements but emphasizes innovative interpretations aimed at the positive aspects of EEO regulations. Figure 3 is a summary flow chart of this procedure.

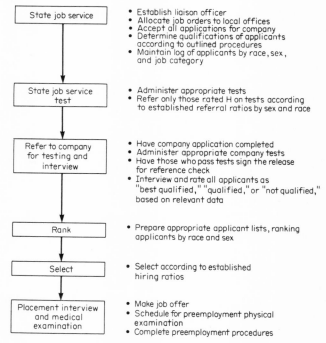

FIG. 3   Model of employee selection procedure.

It will be obvious that these selection procedures have been designed for use in a large company—a company that utilizes the services of the state employment office to prescreen applicants and, in addition, has its own internal preemployment testing program. However, the concept of these procedures applies equally to small organizations as well.

The selection program has been validated and found to be extremely cost-effective. It not only was implemented without incurring additional costs but also actually resulted in *reduced employment-office costs*, and it meets all the requirements of federal regulations.

A word of caution is in order here, however. An organization cannot simply adopt this program with the assumption that it will be valid in its own situation. Quite obviously, any organization would have to formulate its own unique standards and concepts in order to satisfy its own requirements.

(NAME OF COMPANY OR FACILITY)

Employee Selection Procedure

Effective [*date*], the following new-employee selection procedure for entry-level production, maintenance, and clerical positions will be implemented at [*name of company or facility*]. The purpose of the procedure is to enable the company to hire the best candidates available while meeting equal employment opportunity (EEO) obligations. The state employment security administration (ESA) will accept applications from individuals expressing an interest in working for the company and will prescreen, test, and refer applicants to the company according to the procedures outlined herein. Under no circumstances are applications to be received or processed other than according to the following procedure.

Responsibilities and procedures to be followed by the state

1. The state will designate a liaison representative responsible for coordinating the services provided by the ESA. The liaison representative will appoint an assistant to perform liaison duties in his or her absence. All reports, placement of job orders, and investigation and resolution of questions that may occur as a result of this procedure will be handled by the liaison representative. The liaison representative will allocate job orders to the following area offices:

   (List each area office that will be used.)

2. The ESA will accept applications at the designated offices from anyone who wishes to apply with the company and will prescreen, test, and refer applicants for employment according to the following guidelines:

   a. Applicants must meet minimum age standards.

   b. Applicants must have a stable period of employment which means that during the past 5 years the applicant must have:

      (1) Not more than one period of unemployment following a voluntary termination, and the period of unemployment must be of less than 3 months. Breaks in employment, however, resulting from involuntary terminations, such as layoffs or facility closings, should not eliminate applicants from further consideration.

      (2) No termination due to discharge or drop.

   c. If an applicant's work record indicates that he or she has been terminated as the result of a discharge during the last 5 years, the applicant shall not be considered until he or she has reestablished a stable period of employment.

   d. Applicants for production and maintenance positions must be willing to work rotating shifts, weekends, and holidays. Applicants with experience working shifts and weekends and/or experience in production-type positions shall be considered first (this is waived for recent high school students).

   e. Applicants for clerical positions with experience and/or appropriate job-related education and training in white-collar positions shall be considered first.

   f. All other things being relatively equal, applicants who were former employees (i.e., with at least 6 months of company service) shall be given preference.

g. Only applicants who indicate that they missed less than 8 days of work during the prior 12 months of employment shall be referred to the company.[4]

h. If an applicant has been out of school for less than 5 years, his or her high school transcript must show less than an average of 10 days' absence per year.[5]

3. An appropriate, validated test battery, developed in conjunction with the state, shall be administered to all applicants who pass the initial prescreening segment of this procedure. All other things being equal, applicants should be scheduled for testing according to their date of application with the state.

The appropriate clerical aptitude and proficiency tests shall be administered to clerical applicants who pass the initial prescreening segment of this procedure.

The ESA will refer test-qualified applicants to the company according to the following predetermined referral percentages[6]:

Production and Maintenance
White males   _____
Minority males   _____
Females   _____

Clerical
White (male and female)   _____
Minority (male and female)   _____

These referral percentages shall apply to each job order. If the applicant flow should become insufficient to meet these ratios, appropriate recruiting efforts should be initiated to ensure adequate numbers. It should be understood, however, that the distribution of applications should not be restricted to any one of the above categories at any time.

The state may discontinue accepting applications from persons interested in applying for the company whenever a reasonable pool of pretested, prescreened applicants is available (to meet the company's needs). The state will replenish the pool of applicants as needed.

4. The state will maintain a record of persons expressing an interest in applying for employment with the company by race, sex, and job categories for which they are applying. The statistical record of persons applying for employment with the company should be maintained separately by each of the designated offices on a Log and Record of Applicants for Employment. The Log and Record of Applicants for Employment form should provide data on the applicant's race, sex, EEO-1 job choice, and initial and final disposition.

On a monthly basis for the first 6 months after initiation of this employee selection procedure, and quarterly thereafter, the ESA coordinator shall conduct reviews to determine whether adverse impact exists in any of the stages of the initial prescreening of this procedure. Results of the reviews should be forwarded to the company representatives for their review.

---

[4] Specific attendance standards must be established by considering both the average number of occurrences of absenteeism by present employees and any company goals for improving absenteeism.

[5] See footnote 4, above.

[6] Specific referral percentages must be developed by each company location, based on applicant flow, availability, etc.

5. Any questions that arise at any time during the application process pertaining to an applicant's status, handling, or disposition should be referred to the company. If the ESA is unable to meet the established referral ratios for any category(s) for any reasons, it should advise the plant immediately. The state should communicate *only* with the *employment manager* or designated representatives.

Responsibilities and procedures to be followed by the company

1. When the company is in need of applicants for production and maintenance or clerical employment, it shall obtain all applicants from the state ESA. All applicants for the abovementioned positions should be referred to one of the local ESA offices. Even though the company may have a sufficient number of applicants on file to fill a requisition, it is still necessary to register the job opening with the ESA.

2. Applicants referred by the ESA will be asked to complete a company Application for Employment form. All applicants will be listed on the Log and Record of Applicants for Employment maintained by the company.

   Employment applications will be considered active for a period of 1 year[7] from the filing date at the company. If the applicant is not hired or is eliminated during the active period, his or her application will become inactive and remain in the inactive file for 1 year. In order to be reconsidered, a person must reapply through the ESA.

3. Applicants will also be given the appropriate company preemployment test battery. Those who pass the appropriate tests, including any retesting which may be involved, will be asked to sign the Authorization for Release of Information form(s) for reference checks. The completed forms will be mailed to designated former employers.

   If the company receives information from a former employer of an applicant which is adverse to the applicant or which contradicts information contained on the application form, the applicant shall be advised and shall be given an opportunity to clarify the situation. If, after review of the specifics involved in the particular case, it is clear that the applicant falsified the information, the applicant shall not be considered for employment. If the person has already been hired, he or she shall be terminated. Under no circumstances should an applicant for employment be disqualified on the basis of information received from prior employers without being given the opportunity to clarify the information nor should an applicant be disqualified because an employer failed to return a completed form.

4. All applicants who pass the appropriate labor or clerical entry-level test *and* who meet *all* of the following criteria should be scheduled for an employment interview:

   a. The applicant must meet all the prerequisites presented in item 2 of page 105.

   b. The applicant must have a satisfactory attendance record with former employer(s). Failure of a previous employer to provide reference check information will not disqualify an applicant.

   c. The applicant must not have a record of unacceptable termination(s).

---

[7] Active retention periods will vary depending on the demonstrated needs of the company.

   d. The applicant must have appropriate job-related training and/or work experience. Previous training and work experience will be waived for recent high school students.

5. All applicants scheduled for an employment interview should be asked to bring the following document(s) to the interview:

   a. High school transcript, if the person has less than 5 years of work experience.

   b. DD214 (military discharge papers), if the applicant has indicated he or she is a Vietnam-era veteran. (Note: Under no circumstances should discharge papers be copied or retained. The only purpose for reviewing this document is to certify that the person is a qualified Vietnam-era or disabled veteran.)

6. The applicant will be interviewed, and the results will be recorded on the interviewer's report. Based on a review of all relevant data, the interviewer will rate the applicant as either "best-qualified," "qualified," or "not qualified."

   When an applicant reaches the employment interview stage of the selection process, he or she should be considered "qualified." That applicant has passed the tests, demonstrated reasonable job stability, and normally has had some relevant job experiences. But the extent to which the person is a hard worker, able to get along with people, and is reasonably mature is still an unknown. These determinations should be made at the conclusion of a 40-minute, patterned interview conducted by a trained employment interviewer. After reviewing the applicants' work history, education and training, and outside interests, the interviewer must then rate each applicant as "best-qualified," "qualified," or "not qualified."

7. All applicants (best-qualified and qualified) for production and maintenance positions will be placed into one of three categories—white males, minority males, or females. All applicants (best-qualified and qualified) for clerical positions will be placed into one of two categories—whites (males and females) or minorities (males and females). Within each of the above categories, applicants will be ranked in test score order (or by date of employment application at the plant if tests are not used). Preference for selection shall be according to the following criteria:

   a. Applicants rated best-qualified shall be selected for employment first.

   b. Within each category, all other things being relatively equal, applicants who were former employees (specify minimum term to be considered as a former employee) should be selected for employment first.

8. When vacancies occur, the plant will select applicants for employment according to the following minimum hiring goals[8]:

Production and Maintenance	
Minority males	25%
Females	20%

Clerical	
Minorities (males and females)	10%

   Example: 20 plant labor vacancies

   20 x 55% = 11 white males
   20 x 25% =   5 minority males
   20 x 20% =   4 females
   —————
   20 total

---

[8] Specific hiring percentages must be determined for each company location.

The hiring goals, which are interpreted as minimum levels, shall apply to each personnel requisition. If the plant is unable to meet its hiring goals for any category(ies), corrective action should be implemented immediately.

9. Failure of an applicant to report for a scheduled appointment during the selection process or for work without prior notification to the ESA or the plant will result in disqualification for employment consideration.

PART THREE

The Employment Interview

CHAPTER SEVEN

Substance of the Interview

In earlier chapters of this book we have referred to the employment interview as the most important selection procedure. Applicants who have survived the early screening steps are now scheduled for the final interview. This is the most critical aspect of the selection program since it is here that all information obtained from the preliminary interview, the application form, the aptitude tests, and the reference check is integrated with other factors of the individual's background and the final decision is made. Applicants who have survived to this point obviously have something to offer. They have passed the employment tests, they have demonstrated some stability in their employment history, and their previous work history and educational background reflect some degree of relevance in terms of the jobs for which they are being considered. But there are still important questions about these individuals that have not yet been answered. Up to this point, we do not know how diligently they will be willing to work, whether they are likely to get along well with people, whether they can adapt to the environment of the plant or office, and whether they are likely to show up for work every day. It is to these important areas that we address ourselves in the final interview.

UNIQUE FEATURES OF THE FINAL INTERVIEW

We have commented earlier that a vast majority of interviewers are "turned loose" in their jobs without any formal training at all. As a consequence, many interviewers do not interview in accordance with any plan and, hence, do not use their time effectively, many do far too much of the talking themselves, and many, perhaps unconsciously, base their final decision on surface impressions because they do not know how to probe for relevant, hard data.

In the kind of interview described here, we *do* operate according to plan (see the interview guide in the Appendix). We take applicants back to their earlier work experience and proceed chronologically through all their jobs up to their present position or last job. From there we discuss educational background, starting with grammar school or high school and proceeding to the highest grade completed. During all this discussion, we probe for clues to behavior in an effort to get a clear picture of their strengths and shortcomings.

This is the type of interview, moreover, where the applicant has the center of the stage and is encouraged to do most of the talking. Using techniques which are discussed in a subsequent chapter, interviewers develop such a high degree of rapport that applicants talk spontaneously and, hence, usually provide a clear picture of who they are and what they are like deep down inside. In such an interview, interviewers usually find it necessary to talk only about 15 percent of the time. This gives them a first-rate opportunity to sit back and analyze clues to behavior as they are reflected in the applicant's spontaneous remarks.

Unlike interviewers who base their hiring decision on a hunch or surface impressions, we make every effort to *document* our findings with concrete data drawn from the applicant's history. Thus, a finding such as *willingness to work* should be based upon such evidence as early conditioning to work as a young person, long hours spent on certain jobs, "moonlighting" (working on two or more jobs at the same time), or carrying out a substantial (20 hours a week or more) part-time job while carrying a full academic load in school.

PHILOSOPHY OF THE INTERVIEW

Experience has shown that the best way to predict what a person will do in the future is on the basis of what he or she has done in the past. Although it is possible for individuals to grow and develop, and in that way to *modify* their behavior, few people are likely to overcome completely the effect that long years of behaving in a certain manner has produced in them. Hence, if a man has worked hard all his life from the time he was a teenager, he is very likely to work hard for his new employer. And if a woman has shown the ability to adapt to new and changing situations in her previous job experiences, she is more likely to be able to make whatever adjustments may be required in the new job for which she is being considered. Moreover, if she has been able to stay with most of her previous jobs for a reasonable period of time—3 to 5 years—she is quite likely to remain with her new employer for a like period. Finally, if candidates have demonstrated the *ability to get along with people* on previous jobs, in extracurricular activities in school, or in activities outside of work or school, they are very likely to get along well with people in their new plant or office situation.

FUNCTIONS OF THE INTERVIEW

In addition to the integration of all information obtained from previous selection steps, it becomes the function of the interviewer to (1) determine the relevance of an applicant's experience and training in terms of the demands of a specific job, (2) appraise his or her personality, motivation, and character, and (3), in the absence of aptitude tests, evaluate mental ability.

The third factor—mental ability—may not represent an area of great importance in some hourly jobs. In fact, persons with above average intelligence often find routine jobs extremely boring and dissatisfying. On the other hand, most companies prefer to hire individuals with potential for advancement, and here intelligence *does* play an important part. Other factors being reasonably equal, the extent to which an individual is capable of promotion to more complex and demanding jobs is frequently determined by the amount of mental ability he or she possesses. Suggestions for making these determinations appear in later chapters of this book.

Once all these factors have been assessed, the interviewer is in a position to make the final hiring decision. This is of necessity a subjective decision, a decision based upon the interviewer's experience, judgment, and training. But, in this type of interview, the decision should be based on factual evidence rather than the unsupported hunch. In the final analysis, interviewers not only evaluate a candidate's assets and liabilities in terms of the demands of a given job, they must also judge the extent to which the assets *outweigh* the liabilities, or vice versa. Only in this way can they rate applicants as excellent, above average, average, below average, or poor.

In today's market, employers have found that some applicants will do almost anything to get a job. Sometimes this takes the form of exaggerating their accomplishments, putting on an act for the interviewer's benefit, or perhaps downright lying. Hence, interviewers must from the very beginning actively look for *unfavorable* information. Otherwise they may be taken in by surface appearances and behavior. Interviewers are human and thus, despite their efforts to maintain objectivity, react more favorably to some persons than they do to others. When the initial reaction is favorable, interviewers have a natural tendency to look only for those clues which will confirm original impressions. It helps to remember, though, that none of us is perfect; we all have shortcomings. *The interview that results in no unfavorable information is therefore inescapably a poor interview.*

In the final analysis, interviewers are faced with only two broad objectives. They must be able to develop relevant information, and they must be able to interpret the information they bring to light. These objectives are sufficiently complex, however, that the remaining chapters of this book are directed to their accomplishment. The next three chapters are concerned with helping interviewers obtain the necessary information. The final chapters of the book are devoted to interpretation.

CHAPTER EIGHT

How to Develop Rapport— Getting the Applicant to Talk Spontaneously

In far too many interviews, the so-called *question and answer technique* prevails. In such an interview, the interviewer asks the questions; the applicant answers the questions and waits for the next one. This type of interview not only is stilted and mechanical but, more seriously, also gives applicants an opportunity to *screen their replies.* Thus, they're inclined to provide responses which they think will put them in the best light, rather than tell the story as it actually is. Moreover, interviewers do almost half the talking, leaving applicants with that much less of an opportunity to discuss all the relevant aspects of their background.

The question and answer approach to interviewing also tends to take on the aspects of an inquisition. Applicants feel that they are being *grilled* and hence are uncomfortable. As a consequence, they often provide as little information about themselves as possible *and almost never discuss any of their shortcomings.*

In this chapter we will discuss a completely different kind of interview. Instead of putting applicants on the spot, the interviewer should try to develop a harmonious relationship, one in which

117

applicants not only feel comfortable but also develop so much confidence in the interviewer that they begin to talk spontaneously. Instead of waiting for the next question, therefore, they tend to discuss their background with appropriate elaboration, to the extent that their discourse becomes spontaneous. When people talk spontaneously, information seems to well up and bubble out in such a way that there is no need or, indeed, opportunity to screen their replies. Hence, spontaneous information is much more likely to reflect an individual's true feelings, needs, or anxieties, and, more often than not, spontaneous information contains clues to shortcomings. Remember, interviewers must become aware of applicants' shortcomings as well as their assets. Otherwise, not only is it impossible to make appropriate job placements but individuals may be hired for job situations in which they would be incompetent and conceivably quite miserable.

Techniques for developing rapport discussed in this chapter work so well that some applicants tend to talk too much—to the point that the problem becomes one of *controlling* their discourse rather than getting them to open up. Interviewers who take the time to adopt these techniques will discover that they have a completely new tool at their disposal, a tool that will not only help them in the interview but also come to their assistance in many other aspects of their lives. Persons who have learned how to develop rapport become better supervisors, do a better job of feeding back appraisal information, and even become more popular at parties.

SMALL TALK

In any conversation between two people, it is only natural to begin with some pleasantry rather than to delve directly into the purpose of the meeting. As far as the interview is concerned, in fact, this becomes an important aspect of establishing initial rapport. This is the interviewer's first opportunity to get applicants to assume a major portion of the conversational load. If they can be helped to do most of the talking during this early phase of the interview, they naturally assume this to be their role throughout and often fall into this role without any difficulty at all. However, if the small talk revolves around a series of short, direct questions, such as "How was your trip?" it usually leads to a question and answer approach where the interviewer does as much as half the talking. In that case, applicants have the right to assume that their role is one of simply answering any question that may be addressed to them rather than talking spontaneously.

The Importance of Beginning Small Talk
with a General Question

Rather than pose questions that invite short yes or no responses, it is more desirable to use a general "pump-priming" question— one that cannot be answered without a fair amount of discussion. Such questions require preparation, however, and cannot be expected to be phrased on the spur of the moment. Prior to the interview, therefore, the interviewer should study the completed application, in an effort to come up with a topic on which the applicant might be expected to talk freely and perhaps enthusiastically. Such a topic might be concerned with a particular interest, some indicated achievement such as a scholarship, or perhaps differences encountered living in two different parts of the country. The interviewer should be armed with one or two such topics prior to the interview. Whatever the topic, the initial question should be broad enough in nature, so that the applicant will be required to talk 2 or 3 minutes in order to answer it. Several examples of such pump-priming questions are listed below.

1. "I notice from your application that you apparently like to ski. Tell me how you got involved in skiing and where you most enjoy it. What kind of satisfactions do you get out of it?"

2. "In looking over your application, I noticed that you were given an award at the Henry White Company for making a valuable suggestion concerning your work. Tell me what the award involved and what the suggestion accomplished."

3. "I notice from your application that you have worked in California as well as here in the midwest. How do the two areas of the country compare with respect to things like climate, cost of living, recreational opportunities, attitude of the people, that sort of thing?"

Questions such as those listed above are sufficiently complex that it usually requires at least 2 or 3 minutes to answer them. If the applicant stops after a sentence or two, simply wait, drawing upon the technique to be discussed later—the calculated pause. In posing any incidental question designed to promote small talk, interviewers should make an effort to be as pleasant as possible, treating the subject as what it actually is, an "ice breaker," rather than a more serious part of the interview.

As long as the applicant keeps talking, interviewers should not take any part in the discussion at all. They should simply smile, nod their heads, and engage in other nonverbal, supportive behavior discussed later on in this chapter. They should never break in with questions of their own, no matter how interested they may be in the topic under discussion. At this stage of the interview, we do not care at all what applicants say, so long as they take over the conversation. Should their conversation come to a halt, interviewers can perhaps keep it going a little longer by repeating a part of the original broad question which has so far been unanswered. Small talk ranging from 2 to 4 minutes is usually sufficient to ease whatever nervousness an applicant may have initially experienced. The sound of one's own voice in a strange situation usually helps to develop confidence, ease initial tension, and build rapport. When applicants are not immediately put on the spot by being asked to tell about some more serious aspect of their background, they do not feel the need to sell themselves, and, thus, they have the chance to relax and to chat informally about matters which are of no great concern.

THE CALCULATED PAUSE

We have mentioned that interviewers should wait out applicants who stop talking without having answered all parts of a multifaceted question. We call this the *calculated pause*, and we use this as a *conscious technique*. Interviewers without much experience tend to become uncomfortable whenever a slight pause in the conversation occurs and are therefore likely to break in prematurely with unnecessary comments or questions. But experienced interviewers purposely permit a pause to occur from time to time because they know that applicants will frequently elaborate on a previous point rather than allow the discussion to come to a standstill. The applicant often senses that the interviewer's silence calls for a fuller treatment of the topic under consideration.

In the conscious use of the pause, interviewers *must not break eye contact*. If they look down at their guide, applicants naturally assume that they are formulating another question and, hence, wait for that question to be articulated. However, if interviewers do not break eye contact and *look expectant* as the pause elongates, applicants feel a certain degree of pressure and usually search quickly for something else to say. Obviously, if applicants fail to respond within a few seconds, interviewers should relieve the pressure by asking another question. To do otherwise might risk a loss of rapport.

Under normal circumstances, the calculated pause is remarkably effective in drawing out spontaneous information. Equally important, interviewers have to do less talking when they use an occasional pause and, therefore, perfect the art of becoming a good listener.

Once perfected, the calculated pause is a powerful technique, particularly when not used too frequently. It also has wide application outside the interview situation. It is a useful tool for salespeople in determining a customer's needs, it is widely used in the legal profession, and it is a valuable technique for use in labor negotiations in determining what is on the other person's mind.

FACIAL EXPRESSIONS

We have just mentioned that interviewers should *look expectant* as a means of making the calculated pause effective, but looking expectant and being *facially responsive* are conscious techniques that should be utilized throughout the interview. Anyone can manage an expectant look by lifting the eyebrows a little and smiling slightly. This expression gives the interviewer the appearance of being *receptive* and serves as a powerful tool in getting the subject to open up. People who are facially responsive react facially as well as verbally to another individual's comment. When that individual smiles, the interviewer should smile; when the applicant talks about an unfortunate experience, the interviewer's face should show concern.

Facial expressions play a particularly important role when asking questions that border on the personal. The edge is taken off a delicate or personal question when it is posed with a half smile with the eyebrows raised. And, as we shall see later on, facial expressions are of paramount importance in probing for an individual's shortcomings. Finally, facial expressions help to give one the appearance of being understanding, sympathetic, and receptive. There are some individuals, in fact, who are so adroit with facial expressions that they are able to keep the subject talking almost by that means alone. It is a matter of fact that some people's countenances are naturally more animated than others. Thus, some people find it necessary to work at being facially responsive, while others find it very natural.

Persons being trained as interviewers sometimes raise the question, "Isn't it possible that I will look like a phony if I try too hard to become facially responsive?" The answer to this, of course, is a qualified "yes." Facial expressions, as in the case of all other conscious techniques, can be overdone and can give interviewers the appearance of being artificial and insincere. Experience has shown, however, that *most people do not use enough facial expression.* It is the rare person indeed who tends to overplay this aspect of interviewing technique.

When we stop to realize that there are only two means at our disposal in getting through to people in social situations—facial expressions and voice—it certainly behooves all of us to make maximum utilization of whatever talents we have in these two important areas. One has only to look at television programs to note how effective people can be who have had specific training in vocal and facial expression. Although most of us cannot approach this professional level, we can do a lot more with our faces and with our voices than we are currently doing. Conscious effort along these lines can pay big dividends in improved interpersonal relationships.

VOICE

It has often been said that a series of lessons with an elocutionist will enhance anyone's career. This is because people judge us not only by what we say but also by how we say it. In fact, others may not hear what we say if we have not learned how to speak effectively. This is particularly true in the interview situation where we consciously use the voice as a rapport-building technique.

The art of persuasion obviously relies heavily upon the voice. In the interview, we use every means at our disposal to persuade applicants to reveal all their qualifications and characteristics— shortcomings as well as assets. In their attempts to improve vocal effectiveness, interviewers must keep two things in mind: (1) they must not talk too loudly, and (2) they should try to use all *ranges of the voice.* When interviewers talk too loudly, they tend to threaten applicants to some extent and to push them off the center of the stage. Since we expect applicants to do some 85 percent of the talking, they must be "front and center" during the entire interview. When interviewers talk too loudly, they tend to relegate the candidate to a minor role. Since we do not want that to happen, we, as interviewers, try to keep our voices at a rather low conversational level, in that way encouraging the applicant to take over.

It is much easier to teach people to speak more softly than it is to teach them to use all ranges of their voices. In particular, interviewers should concentrate on greater utilization of the upper range of the voice. When we ask applicants questions or give them compliments, for example, we should try to use the upper range of the voice. This has the effect of making us sound more interested in what the other person may have to say, and, in turn, that person becomes more highly motivated to give us the answer we seek and does a more complete job of revealing innermost thoughts.

As in the case of facial expressions, vocal intonations should mirror the applicant's moods. When applicants discuss unfortunate or unhappy aspects of their background, the interviewer's voice should take on a sympathetic tone, and when applicants divulge something of a highly personal nature, the interviewer's voice should reflect an understanding quality. Complete responsiveness on the part of the interviewer has an unusually powerful effect upon the other person, making that individual not only willing but often actually anxious to talk about things that are uppermost in her or his mind.

Of course, vocal inflection can be overdone. This should be avoided at all costs because it gives the impression of insincerity and may have the effect of alienating individuals rather than attracting them. Again, though, it is the rare individual who falls into this trap. Most of us do not use sufficient vocal intonation and hence could profit from training in this area. For many years, the General Electric Company has sponsored a course called "Effective Presentation." This course has become one of the most popular courses in the GE training program, with some people finding it so helpful that they have taken it a second time. Interviewers would be well-advised to take courses of this nature if such courses exist in their organization.

LUBRICATION, OR REINFORCEMENT

There is perhaps no more powerful tool in the interviewer's arsenal than that of commenting positively on an applicant's achievements. Some people in the field refer to this as "stroking," some call it "reinforcement," and others just refer to it as "giving an applicant a pat on the back." We like to think of it as "lubrication." Just as a drop of oil from time to time keeps a piece of machinery running, so do positive comments interspersed throughout the interview help to maintain rapport and keep applicants talking. For years, psychologists have experimented with some system of reward to train both animals in the laboratory and human beings. For example, reinforcement, or some system of reward, has proved effective in training retarded children to dress and feed themselves.

In the interview situation, lubrication, or reinforcement, can be both verbal and nonverbal. Comments such as "Very impressive!" or "You deserve a lot of credit for that!" or "Excellent!" give applicants the feeling that their achievements are being appropriately recognized, and they respond accordingly. Such achievements as (1) high grades in school, (2) promotion on the job, (3) unusually long hours spent on a given job, (4) election to class office, or (5) being invited back for a second summer of part-time work merit favorable recognition on the part of the interviewer. When achievements of this kind are recognized by interviewers in the form of a compliment, applicants often visibly warm to the discussion and become increasingly expansive and spontaneous in their ensuing remarks. To be appreciated is a human need, and the job applicant is no exception in this respect.

Few people realize, however, that lubricating responses can be *nonverbal* as well as verbal. Frequent nodding of the head and sounds of affirmation such as "Uh huh" and "Hmmm" help applicants feel that interviewers are paying attention to their discourse and appreciate what they are saying. Actually, one-word interjections such as "Fine!", "Terrific!", or "Impressive!" can be worked into the discussion without interrupting the applicant at all. The frequency with which forms of lubrication are utilized during the interview depends largely on the applicant's makeup. If the person is a relatively sophisticated, secure individual, a considerable amount of lubrication would not be appropriate. In such a case, nonverbal reinforcement and a few verbalized comments would normally be sufficient. If an applicant is insecure and relatively unsophisticated, a great deal more lubrication would be in order.

As noted earlier, intonation plays an important part in supportive comments. When the voice is consciously placed in the upper register, rather than mumbled or "swallowed," the comment takes on greater significance. It has the effect of making the interviewer sound more impressed with the applicant's achievement. This has the long-range effect of building so much rapport that applicants become subsequently more willing to discuss some of their shortcomings. People do not mind talking about some of their problems if they are absolutely certain that the listener is completely aware of their successes.

PLAYING DOWN UNFAVORABLE INFORMATION

Just as we compliment applicants on their achievements, so do we *play down* their problems or difficulties. This is done to make it easier for individuals to talk about negative aspects of their backgrounds, and since we are searching for shortcomings as well as assets, this becomes an important part of our interview technique. Playing down takes the form of some casual, understanding remark. If, for example, a woman talks about the "terrible time she had with mathematics in school," this can be played down by such a sympathetic remark as, "All of us have different aptitudes; the chances are that you may have been a lot stronger in the verbal area." Or, if a young man admits a lack of self-confidence, we might say, "Self-confidence is a trait that most people develop as a result of living a little longer and acquiring more experience."

When applicants discuss unfavorable information of a more serious nature, such as poor attendance on a previous job or a fiery temper, a casual, sympathetic remark on the part of the interviewer would *not* be appropriate. In such a case, it is better to compliment the individual for being able to recognize the problem and face up to it. An appropriate comment might be, "The fact that you are aware of this situation and have been able to face up to it means that you have already taken the first step toward doing something about it." Such a statement by no means makes light of the individual's problem but does provide a pat on the back for being able to face up to it, and this is usually enough to make a person feel better about having revealed the difficulty.

There is one further thing to keep in mind. Interviewers should *never tell applicants anything that is untrue.* If a person should admit to a lack of initiative, for example, one would never say, "Oh, that is something you should be able to overcome very easily." Since traits of this kind tend to become quite deeply imbedded in the personality structure, they are *not* easily overcome. Most applicants would be aware of this and hence would detect the ring of insincerity in an interviewer's comment.

We would like to emphasize once again, though, the importance of playing down unfavorable information. The interviewer who gives the slightest indication that judgment is being adversely influenced by unfavorable information will get no further information of this kind. Once interviewers react negatively—either verbally or facially—they disqualify themselves as sympathetic listeners. No one willingly and spontaneously talks about difficulties and failures in a climate where the listener does not give the appearance of being understanding. On the other hand, when such information is not only accepted without surprise or disapproval but also played down, the applicant is permitted to *save face* and hence usually finds it easy to discuss additional negative data if this should be part of his or her history.

COMPREHENSIVE INTRODUCTORY QUESTIONS

Although the first comprehensive introductory question is asked immediately after small talk, we are discussing this technique at the very end of this chapter in order to give it emphasis. The comprehensive introductory question represents *the single most important technique for getting applicants to do most of the talking.* This type of question is so comprehensive, in fact, that many applicants can talk several minutes and still not answer all aspects of the question.

Once the small talk has come to an end, interviewers bridge the gap between the small talk and the first introductory question with a comment such as, "Let me tell you a little bit about our discussion today." They then direct the conversation to the real purpose of the session by making an appropriate *opening remark*. This general opening remark should include a statement of the company's interest in placing new employees in jobs that make the best use of their ability. It should present an *overview* of the interview by pointing out that the discussion will include as much relevant information as possible about work history, education, and interests. A question such as the following will usually suffice: *"In this company, we believe that the more information we can obtain about persons applying for work the better able we will be to place them in a job that makes best use of their abilities. I would therefore like to have you tell everything you can about your work experience, education and training, and present interests."*

Having provided the applicant with the discussion of the purpose of the interview and having given an overview of the general topics to be considered, the interviewer launches immediately into a discussion of previous work experience, the first topic that appears on the interview guide (see Appendix). This is accomplished with the first comprehensive introductory question, for example, *"Suppose you begin by telling me about your previous jobs, starting with the first job and working up to the present. I would be interested in how you got each job, your duties and responsibilities, the level of earnings, your job likes and dislikes, and any special achievements along the way."* The very comprehensiveness of this question provides applicants with a basis for a considerable amount of discussion and, as indicated above, represents the single most important factor in getting them to talk for as much as 85 percent of the interview time.

After the work experience has been completed, interviewers should launch into the second topic for discussion—education. A question such as the following will do the job here: *"Suppose you tell me now about your education, starting with the earlier grades and working up through high school. [Use the word "college" when appropriate.] I would be interested in the subjects you liked best, those you did not care so much for, the level of your grades, your extracurricular activities, and any special academic achievements. What subjects did you like best in high school?"*

We do not expect applicants to remember every single item in the introductory question. They will very often have to be reminded, for example, to discuss subject preferences or asked to talk at greater length about extracurricular activities. Such followup questions, though, are simply *reminders* of some of the things applicants have been initially asked to talk about. As such, they do not represent new questions and hence do not require quite so much concentration on the applicant's part.

The Importance of Memorization

Interviewers are advised to *memorize verbatim* the questions presented above. This will make their interviews a lot smoother, and because they do not have to concern themselves with formulating such questions, they are much more free to *listen* to what applicants have to say.

Assume Consent

In verbalizing introductory questions, interviewers should use every means at their disposal to *sell* candidates on the desirability of providing the necessary information. In particular, they should consciously use appropriate facial expressions and vocal intonations. And their very manner should *assume consent*. Just as an effective salesperson assumes that the customer wants to buy, so the expert interviewer assumes that applicants will be happy to respond to all of his or her questions. Questions are best phrased *positively,* in such a way that there is no alternative but to answer them. The phrase "suppose you tell me" is always more effective than the phrase "I wonder if you would be willing to tell me." The latter choice of words provides the alternative of not answering and thus fails to assume consent. Also, it gives the impression that the interviewer is not confident and thus may not be certain whether or not he or she should ask the question.

The techniques discussed in this chapter are almost foolproof in terms of getting spontaneous information and getting the applicant to do the major share of the talking. Interviewers, in fact, who study these techniques carefully and use them as described here will often be quite amazed how productive they can be.

EEO AREAS OF CONCERN

1. Do not overdo rapport-getting techniques with minorities or women. This is not necessary, and they will be quick to discern the special treatment.

2. Do not assume a "holier than thou" attitude or "talk down" to the applicant. Interviewer and interviewee must be on the same wavelength.

3. Be careful about informal chitchat before beginning the interview proper. Interviewers have been known to make such statements as, "I have a daughter about your age, and I can't imagine her wanting to work in this industry."

4. Informal talk at the end of the interview can also create problems. There have been instances where interviewers began talking about sports but, without being aware of the impression they were making, ended up by taking a stand on racial issues. As soon as the interview has been completed, thank the applicant, say you will be in touch with him or her, and stand up as an indication that the discussion has been concluded.

5. Minorities and females who anticipate a negative hiring decision monitor the interviewer's facial expression very closely. In such cases, therefore, interviewers should try all the harder to mask their true reactions. Facial expressions that reflect a negative reaction have been known to lead to charges of discrimination. In these cases applicants charge that the interviewer was biased—that they "never had a chance."

6. Never patronize members of a protected group (minorities, females, or the handicapped) by indicating in any way that they are being hired because the company has an EEO program. Such a statement may lead applicants to believe that they are not being hired on the basis of their qualifications, and people do not like to think that they have been accepted only because standards have been lowered or rules have been bent.

CHAPTER NINE

How to Probe for Clues to Behavior

Most interviews, in the hands of untrained interviewers, are little more than *surface* discussions—discussions that seldom reveal what a person is like deep down inside. This is why attempts to validate the interview as a selection device have seldom shown positive results. Most interviewers do not get a truly clear picture of such important factors as an applicant's motivation, level of maturity, or basic intelligence. The untrained interviewer simply does not possess the *tools* to probe for important factors of this kind.

In this chapter, therefore, we will make every attempt to supply these tools—in the form of probing questions that have been developed over a lifetime of interviewing. Some of these questions appear on the interview guide and should be used verbatim. It is suggested that interviewers make a lap for themselves by crossing their legs and placing the interview guide on the knee. This position makes it easy for them to refer to the guide constantly and read the questions off of the guide verbatim.

In the previous chapter we presented comprehensive introductory questions designed to launch the discussion in each area of the interview, but those questions, of course, will by no means do the entire job. Interviewers must use so-called *follow-up questions* —questions that follow the comprehensive introductory question —to keep applicants talking and to probe more deeply for clues to behavior. Actually, follow-up questions represent an extension of the comprehensive introductory question. They are used to prod applicants from time to time, in this way helping them to reveal their life story to the fullest extent and to become more definitive concerning its important aspects. Actually, interviewers' remarks should be interjected so artfully that the interviewers seldom, if ever, assume the center of the stage. Rather, they dart in and out with such facility that applicants seldom become aware of the fact that their discourse is being directed.

Comments Are Often More Natural Than Questions

Since interviewing also represents *conversation* between two people, comments are usually more natural than questions. Whenever a comment can be substituted for a question, in fact, conversation flows more smoothly and interviewers lessen the impression of being *investigative* in their approach. If they want more information on a given subject, they can frequently get such information by the simple comment, "That sounds very interesting." So encouraged, the applicant is quite likely to provide further elaboration without having been specifically asked to do so. We do not want to give the impression here that there is anything wrong with asking questions. Comments interspersed with questions, however, provide more variety and help the interview to seem more natural.

Keep Questions and Comments Open-Ended

There is a great tendency for interviewers to put words in the applicant's mouth by asking leading questions or making leading comments. By so doing, they unintentionally structure their remarks so that a favorable response is strongly suggested. A comment such as, "I suppose you found that job very boring," pushes the applicant to answer in the affirmative even though that may not have been the case at all.

A leading question such as, "Did you rank pretty high in your high school class?" makes it difficult for the applicant to give a negative response. Since the interviewer has asked a leading question, the applicant is greatly tempted to say "Yes." The applicant whose grades were poor, and who honestly admits it, may realize at once that this could create a negative impression and may become uncomfortable in the interview situation and unwilling to offer any more potentially negative information.

In order to avoid such leading comments or questions, the interviewer should keep remarks *open-ended*. An open-ended question is one that does not telegraph an anticipated response, leaving the applicant free to discuss favorable or unfavorable information. A question such as, "What about grades in high school," gives no clue at all as to the weight which the interviewer may place on grades. In such a question, applicants are free to structure the reply themselves, pointing out that their grades may have been average, above average, or even below average.

There is a wonderful phrase—"To what extent"—that makes any question open-ended. Instead of using a leading question such as, "Were you successful on that job?" the question can be open-ended by saying, *"To what extent* were you successful on that job?" Or, instead of saying, "Did you *enjoy* that experience?" one might say, *"To what extent* did you find that experience satisfying?" in that way converting the question to an open-ended situation.

There is another remarkably effective way to ensure an open-ended response—the use of the question, "How did you *feel about* that situation?" When you say, "Did you *like* the people there?" you push the person to say "Yes." But, when you say, "How did you *feel about* the people there?" you can anticipate an objective response.

Talk the Applicant's Language

There is no quicker way to lose rapport than to use words which are outside the applicant's vocabulary. The applicant becomes quickly confused and is made to feel inferior. Interviewers who are good listeners can determine an applicant's range of vocabulary in a relatively short period of time and subsequently make every effort to use verbiage which the applicant readily understands.

Questions and Comments
Must Be Work-Related

If we are to stay within EEO guidelines, our questions must be primarily concerned with the relevance of an applicant's work history and education to the job under consideration. Our primary concern has to do with the extent to which applicants can handle a job and will make mature, stable employees. As mentioned in previous chapters, we no longer ask about specific age, marital status, number of dependents, or personal finances.

At the same time, we do still have the right to determine *how well* applicants have performed on their previous jobs or in school. This is obviously work-related because it provides strong clues concerning an individual's ability to handle a job for which he or she is being considered. If there is a consistency of good performance on previous jobs, it can be assumed that good performance may be expected on a new job.

PROBING MORE DEEPLY
FOR CLUES TO BEHAVIOR

We mentioned previously that many interviewers fail to probe beneath the surface because they do not have the tools to do the job. The material that follows provides such tools in the form of three kinds of extremely important questions.

The Laundry List Question

Applicants almost invariably find some areas more difficult to discuss than others. Confronted with a question that requires considerable analysis, they frequently "block" and find it somewhat difficult to come up with an immediate response. In such a situation, the interviewer comes to the applicant's assistance with a *laundry list*-type question. As the name implies, this kind of question suggests a variety of possible responses and permits subjects to take their choice. If candidates block on the question, "What are some of the things that a job has to have to give you satisfaction?" the interviewer may stimulate thinking by such a laundry list comment as, "Well, you know some people are more interested in money, some want security, some look for the satisfaction of working with their hands, others enjoy working as a member of a team, and others like a job that takes them out of doors a good bit of the time. What's important to you?" Given a variety of possible responses, applicants are normally able to get their thoughts together and supply a considerable amount of information.

Laundry list questions can also be used as a means of confirming clues to behavior that interviewers have obtained from previous aspects of a discussion. Let us assume, for example, that an applicant has dropped some hints that seem to indicate a dislike for repetitive work. Interviewers can follow up on such clues by including a reference to repetitive work in a laundry list question at the end of the work history section of the interview. They might say, for example, "What are some other things that a job has to have to give you satisfaction? Some people like a fair amount of detail while others do not; some adjust very well to work of a repetitive nature while others find this difficult to take; some like to work with their hands while others prefer paperwork or working with figures. What's important to you?"

If, in response to the above question the candidate says, "Well, I certainly do not want anything that involves a lot of repetition; that type of work drives me up a tree," the interviewer would certainly have obtained further confirmation of the original clue. The very fact that the individual selected this item for a discussion reflects the importance he or she attaches to it. If such an applicant were being considered for a job that was quite routine, the response could be interpreted as revealing a relatively serious shortcoming for the job under consideration.

Most important of all, laundry list questions represent an adroit method of getting applicants to reveal themselves without asking about specific traits. At some point in the interview, for example, applicants may be asked about their strengths. Instead of asking the individual whether he or she is a hard worker, interviewers bury this item in a laundry list question such as the following: "What did you learn about your strengths? Did you find that you perhaps work a little harder than the average person, get along better with people, organize things better, have a better attendance record—just what?" If individuals *select* from such a question an item such as ability to work hard, their response becomes more meaningful because they have volunteered it spontaneously.

Laundry list questions have the added value of spelling out to the applicant what interviewers specifically have in mind. By the very nature of the items used in the series of possible responses, interviewers encourage the applicant to respond specifically rather than generally. In the question noted above, for example, where asked to talk about his or her strengths, the applicant would probably have been at something of a loss unless the question was followed by a laundry list of possible responses, thereby directing the discussion specifically rather than generally.

"Why" Questions

Experienced interviewers know that *why* an individual took some course of action is frequently more revealing than *what* he or she did. This is true because why people do things tells us a great deal about their judgment, their motivation, and other factors of their personality structure. Probing for why an applicant left a given job, for example, may provide clues to such factors as inability to relate to authority (problems with the boss), inability to adjust to routine work, dissatisfaction with close supervision, or the kind of restlessness that motivates a person to move on to something new. When applicants leave a job before obtaining another one, a why question may reveal a tendency to rationalize, to try to explain away one's failure. A reply such as, "I couldn't very well look for a new job while working 8 hours a day on the present job," taken even at face value indicates poor judgment and immaturity. But it also may be a cover for precipitative action based on a quick temper or even for having been fired.

It is not only important to find out what applicants liked or disliked about their job but perhaps more important still to learn the why of their likes or dislikes. This is what is meant by probing more deeply. If a woman indicates that she liked working with computers, a why question such as, "What is there about working with computers that appeals to you?" would be in order. Such a question may reveal that she has a flair for mathematics, that she enjoys problem solving, that she appreciates the accuracy and thoroughness that are a part of such detailed work, or that she enjoys an opportunity to work on her own without close supervision. When a man indicates a dislike of mathematics in school, a question such as, "What was there about math that turned you off?" would be in order. A reply such as, "I never could understand what I was supposed to do," could conceivably provide a clue to mental ability.

When a woman, for example, indicates that she has an *ability to get along with people*, the interviewer should dig deeper by saying, "What traits do you have that make it possible for you to get along with people as well as you do?" The reply to that question may reveal such valuable traits as tact, empathy, or sensitivity to the needs of others.

It is suggested that why questions be used sparingly throughout the interview. For one thing, there is not sufficient time to probe for the why of everything the applicant says. Also, too frequent use of this technique puts too much pressure on the applicant and results in the feeling that he or she is being grilled. Hence, the technique must be reserved for probing in the most fruitful areas. These areas obviously differ from person to person, but with practice and experience interviewers will learn how to recognize fruitful areas for further probing when they occur.

Double-Edged Questions

Double-edged questioning is used to make it easy for applicants to admit their shortcomings and to help them achieve greater self-insight. The questions are double-edged in the sense that they make it possible for the subject to choose between two possible responses. Moreover, the first alternative is usually phrased in such a way that the subject would not choose that alternative without feeling possessed of the ability or personality trait in question to a fairly high degree. The second alternative is phrased so that it is easy for the applicant to choose that alternative, even though it is the more undesirable of the two possible responses. Hence, this type of question is used only to probe for shortcomings.

Having asked applicants to reveal their strengths, one can logically follow up with a question about their shortcomings. A question about shortcomings can be presented as a laundry list question, with the double-edged question used as a follow-up. Thus, an interviewer might say, "What are some of the things about yourself that you would like to improve? Would you like to develop more self-confidence, acquire more tact, learn to control your temper better, improve your attendance record—just what?" If the applicant finds it difficult to answer this question, the interviewer may probe more specifically with a *double-edged* question such as, *"What about tact; do you have as much of that as you would like to have, or is this something you could improve a little bit?"* Given something specific to talk about, most applicants tend to respond quite spontaneously and often reveal a good bit about their shortcomings.

In interviewing persons for office jobs, interviewers often find a double-edged question such as, "What about your ability to spell; do you have that ability to the extent that you would like, or is that something you could improve a little bit?" quite revealing. How confident the individual may be in her or his ability to spell is often revealed in tone of voice or facial expressions. If there is any hesitancy in the reply or if the person frowns, this may be indicative of a problem area. The point here, though, is that the double-edged question was used to launch this discussion. Most people find it much easier to discuss things that they could *improve* rather then qualities that they *lack*. Thus phrased, the double-edged question represents an adroit way to introduce the subject of shortcomings.

How to Soften Direct Questions

In their efforts to probe more deeply for clues to behavior, some interviewers tend to be too blunt and direct in their questioning. Since this risks a possible loss of rapport, many such questions can be softened by the use of appropriate *introductory phrases* and *qualifying words*. Such introductory phrases as the following will help to soften almost any direct question:

> Is it possible that. . . ?
> How did you happen to. . . ?
> Has there been any opportunity to. . . ?
> To what do you attribute. . . ?

Qualifying words and phrases such as "might," "perhaps," "to some extent," "somewhat," and "a little bit" are also effective in softening direct questions.

A study of the two types of questions listed below will reveal the extent to which the direct question has been softened by means of introductory phrases and qualifying words. The questions on the left are obviously too direct; those on the right are more appropriate.

Too Direct

1. Why did you leave that job?

2. Why do you think you had trouble with your boss?

3. How much money did you save that summer?

4. Why did you decide to take a cut in pay in order to get transferred to that other job?

5. Do you lack self-confidence?

6. Are you overly sensitive?

More Appropriate

1. *How did you happen to* leave that job?

2. *To what do you attribute* the *minor* difficulties you experienced with your supervisor?

3. *Was there any opportunity* to save *any* money that summer?

4. *What prompted your decision* to take a cut in pay in order to get transferred to that other job?

5. Is self-confidence *perhaps* a trait that you might improve *to some extent?*

6. *Is it possible* that you *may* be *somewhat* overly sensitive to criticism?

EEO AREAS OF CONCERN

1. Keep questions job-related.

2. Do not ask questions of minorities or females that you would not ask of nonminorities or males.

3. Never ask questions out of curiosity alone. All questions should have a valid purpose.

4. Never ask a single female about her plans for marriage.

5. Never ask a female if she has someone to care for her children while she works or what her plans are for having children.

6. Do not ask an older worker how many more years he or she plans to work. This could be construed as age discrimination.

7. If the job involves travel, working long hours, or potential transfer, attitudes toward such conditions cannot be asked of females alone. If this question is to be used, it must be used with *all* applicants—males and females alike.

CHAPTER TEN

How to Control the Interview

We mentioned in an earlier chapter that techniques designed to get spontaneous information often work so well that the problem becomes one of *controlling* the applicants' discourse rather than getting them to provide further information. Obviously, getting spontaneous information is the first objective in any interview, for without that there is little to interpret and hence little or no way to discover what the individual is like. Spontaneous discourse in itself, however, is not sufficient. The discussion must be guided and channeled in such a way that applicants discuss what the interviewer wants to learn rather than simply what they themselves want to relate. This requires a subtle form of control.

Teaching interviewers how to exercise optimum control represents one of the most difficult tasks in the entire training procedure. During the early stages of their training, interviewers invariably exercise too little control. In their desire to get spontaneous information, they are inclined to let applicants go on and on, just as long as they talk freely. At that stage of their training, they are often afraid to direct the conversation for fear that such direction might inhibit the flow of conversation. As a result of this completely permissive approach, applicants often are allowed to ramble excessively in discussing their backgrounds and to go into too much detail on topics that may not be particularly relevant. As a consequence, the interview suffers from lack of intensive coverage in the important areas and from lack of balance—too much emphasis on one area of the applicant's background and too little on other areas. In addition, such an interview takes far too much time.

With proper training, though, interviewers gradually learn to use just the right amount of guidance and control, and they learn to do this tactfully and unobtrusively. In the very early stages of the interview, they permit applicants to talk quite freely, even though some of the resulting information may not be particularly relevant. They do this in order to *set the pattern* of letting candidates do most of the talking. Once this pattern has been established, though, they do not hesitate to interject comments and questions at critical points, in order to ensure intensive coverage and sufficient penetration in each area of the applicant's background.

WHY CONTROL IS NECESSARY

As noted above, measures of control are designed to (1) ensure adequate coverage of each area of the applicant's background, (2) secure appropriate penetration into the truly salient aspects of the candidate's previous experiences, and (3) utilize the interviewer's time efficiently and economically.

Appropriate Coverage

Some applicants build up such a head of steam that they tend to *take over the interview* and run away with it. In so doing, they may skip over some important areas too quickly and leave out other factors entirely. They tend to discuss only what they want to tell rather than what the interviewer needs to know.

When applicants begin to take charge and to race over their history too rapidly, the interviewer should step in and control the situation, tactfully reminding such a person to discuss likes and dislikes on each job, reason for leaving, and the like. Otherwise the individual could conceivably cover an entire area such as work experience in as few as 10 minutes, without providing any real clues to behavior or any substantial information about accumulated skills.

The real challenge of interviewing is to get maximum coverage in the shortest period of time. In order to do this, interviewers direct the discussion with the image of the job and worker specifications uppermost in mind. Since they have by far the better knowledge of the job requirements, they are responsible for leading the discussion into the most fruitful areas. If interviewers know, for example, that a given job requires a fair amount of mathematical facility, they will make sure that applicants cover such factors as math grades, amount of study time required to obtain those grades, and how applicants evaluate their own ability in the mathematical area.

Penetration

When interview discussion is not controlled, the resulting formation tends to be too *descriptive* rather than *evaluative*. Applicants may go on and on about their job duties, their employer's share of the market, and products manufactured (all descriptive information) without ever bringing themselves into the picture—their likes, achievements, dislikes, and difficulties (evaluative information). Every interview of course contains a fair amount of descriptive information, particularly during the early stages when applicants are encouraged to talk freely and spontaneously.

As the interview continues, however, interviewers should begin to exercise sufficient control in order to get more and more evaluative information. By means of artful and tactful questioning, they must *penetrate* to the candidate's basic reactions to key situations, with a view to determining what those reactions reveal about the individual's basic makeup.

Economy of the Interviewer's Time

An interview with a candidate for an hourly job in the plant or office usually requires 35 to 45 minutes. In order to accomplish this task within this period of time interviewers actually have to "fight the clock." They should therefore have a clock on their desk in order to keep track of elapsed time and to determine how much more time they can afford to spend on a given area. Actually, they should look at the clock every 4 or 5 minutes, in order to make certain that they are utilizing their time efficiently and effectively.

TECHNIQUES OF CONTROL

It is one thing to talk about the needs for control and quite another to discuss how it can be accomplished. Fortunately, though, we have two effective techniques to draw upon for this purpose: (1) the interview guide and (2) interruption.

Interview Guide

Many inexperienced interviewers approach the interview with no plan at all. They simply pick out some item on the application and go on from there. Such interviews usually suffer from inefficiency and ineffectiveness. Applicants tend to ramble in their discussion and fail to cover some of the more important aspects of their backgrounds.

The interview guide, found in the Appendix of this book, provides a "track to run on" and hence represents a very important aspect of control. This guide can bring order, system, and intensive coverage to a discussion that might otherwise have been inconclusive. The interview guide not only specifies the sequence of the discussion but also includes important factors to be taken up in each major area. The guide is so important that interviewers are advised to keep this form on their laps and refer to it every 2 or 3 minutes throughout the interview. This permits the interviewer to use questions on the form verbatim and ensures against omission of important items.

After they have used the guide for awhile, some interviewers feel that they no longer need it. However, as soon as they put it out of sight, they invariably leave out some important aspect of the candidate's background. No matter how much experience interviewers may have, therefore, they should always operate with the guide before them.

Some interviewers also feel self-conscious about reading questions off the form and hence try to paraphrase these questions, using their own words. This is a mistake in two respects. In the first place, experience has shown that reading questions from the interview guide does not disturb applicants in the least. In the second place, most interviewers find it very difficult to formulate questions on the spur of the moment that are as effective as the questions printed on the guide.

Interruption

When an applicant begins to talk too much—particularly in terms of irrelevant detail and descriptive information—we must control the interview by means of *interruption*. Interruption represents a very effective means of control, but this technique must be employed so subtly that applicants do not realize that they are being interrupted. In order to accomplish this, we draw upon two additional techniques: *timing* and *lubrication*. It is of course impolite to interrupt people in the middle of a sentence, and, yet, if we wait until the end of a sentence, they will already have launched into the next sentence by the time we get around to interrupting them. Hence, we must *time* the interruption to be introduced before they have actually completed the sentence. We therefore interrupt as soon as they have completed a thought but *before they have had a chance to complete the sentence*. When we do interrupt, moreover, we always do so with a lubricating comment such as, "That's very interesting," or, "That must have been very satisfying." The lubricating comment represents the introduction to the comment that will redirect the discussion and move applicants along to another topic. If, for example, an applicant tells too much about his or her likes on a given job, the interviewer may say, "You must have found that very satisfying. Tell me about some of the things you did not like quite so well."

As will be noted from the above, timing means *anticipating the end of a thought* and lubrication in this sense means *making a positive or favorable comment*. Utilization of these two techniques tends to soften the interruption in such a way that applicants may not even realize that they are being interrupted. Because interviewers have commented favorably on a given topic under discussion, applicants are willing to relinquish that topic and permit themselves to be redirected to a new subject.

Interviewers should not be too hasty in interrupting applicants when they wander off the track or go into a bit too much detail, because hasty interruption risks the loss of rapport. Give individuals a minute or two to get the uninteresting or irrelevant topic "off their chests" before shutting them off and redirecting their conversation.

Let us assume that a male applicant, for example, races lightly over his first two or three jobs, apparently thinking that they are not germane to the discussion. Since this would normally occur at the very beginning of the interview and since we want to establish a pattern of having an applicant carry the conversational ball, we would let him talk for 3 or 4 minutes, then, just as he was about to put a period at the end of a sentence, we would inject a positive comment and redirect him to a more thorough treatment of his first job. We might say in this instance, "You have certainly had some interesting early experiences—so interesting in fact that I would like to know more about them. Suppose you tell me more about your likes, dislikes, and earnings on that first job."

Let us take another example, where an applicant, a woman, perhaps, conceivably wanders off the track and launches prematurely into another interview area. In response to our question, "What did you like best on that job," she might reply, "I enjoyed the calculations. You know, I am very good in math. I won the math prize in high school and did exceptionally well in calculus. Our high school had two very fine math teachers, and I learned a lot in their classes." If this woman was not interrupted, she might very easily go on to further discussion of her high school experience and forget all about the discussion of her various jobs. After she has been given a minute or two to discuss her mathematical proficiencies, therefore, we interrupt by anticipating the end of one of her thoughts with a comment such as, "I think it's great that you have such an interest and aptitude in math—particularly since you want to become a systems analyst. Tell me about some of the other things you liked on that job with Moseley and Sons." Because we have not interrupted this woman in the *middle* of a thought and because we have commented favorably about her mathematical proficiency, she would normally be quite willing to be redirected back to her work experience.

The Importance of Interviewing Manner

Despite the fact that interviewers only do about 15 percent of the talking, they nevertheless guide the discussion by their very manner and by the way they carry out their role. Although they are friendly, disarming, and permissive, there is a point beyond which they cannot be pushed. By means of vocal and facial expressions, they assume consent. This means that they ask their questions and make their comments in such a way that the applicant is expected to answer. This inner firmness creates an atmosphere of "remote control." Thus, interviewers take active control only when they have to, but they are always ready to step in when the occasion demands. Since interviewers are already in the power position—it is the applicant who is seeking the job—they can usually maintain control in a very unobtrusive fashion.

Upon occasion, one meets an applicant who is inclined to be facetious. Such a person may make light of some of the interviewer's questions or may even challenge their relevancy. Such a situation obviously requires firmer control. When a question is challenged or treated facetiously, interviewers should simply restate the question, giving their reasons for asking it. By their general manner rather than by anything they say, interviewers underscore their seriousness of purpose. This approach almost invariably prevails, the applicant becoming very cooperative thereafter. Some applicants like to test the interviewer, just to see how far they can go. Once they determine the point beyond which they cannot go, they usually become very cooperative.

OTHER FACTORS OF CONTROL

Applicants obviously vary widely with respect to their interview behavior. It is therefore impossible to discuss all situations where control may be necessary, but there are some general rules that may be applied in almost every case.

Develop Information Chronologically and Systematically

Applicants, of course, are given considerable freedom in their choice of subject matter, but they should nevertheless be encouraged to supply information chronologically and systematically. In discussing their work experience, for example, they should be asked to start with the very first job and work up to their most recent experience. This not only gives a sense of order to this segment of the interview but also makes it easier for the interviewer to ascertain the applicant's vocational achievements over the years. In the educational area, it is always best to start with the first years of high school and go on to the subsequent years or even to college if that level of education has been attained. This gives interviewers an opportunity to see how applicants fare as they progress to more difficult academic subject matter and have to compete with more able individuals. (Many of the less gifted persons drop out of high school after a year or two.) The interview guide, of course, spells out the indicated chronology.

Exhaust Each Area before Going On to the Next One

Constant reference to the interview guide helps interviewers to get all important information in one area before going on to the next. One might find, for example, after completing the work history that he or she has neglected to determine an applicant's earnings. The interviewer should go back and get this information before launching into education.

When an applicant is permitted to crisscross between areas, it becomes very difficult for interviewers to evaluate total achievement in one area. Moreover, after the applicant has left the room, they invariably find that they have forgotten to get some important bit of information.

When omissions do occur and when interviewers do not become aware of this until they are midway in the next area, they should complete the discussion in the current area before going back to get the desired information. To interrupt in the middle of a discussion of education in order to get job earnings breaks the applicant's train of thought and makes it more difficult later for him or her to resume the discussion of education at the point at which it was interrupted.

With Older Applicants, Emphasize Recent Positions

With applicants 35 years old or older, there is little point in developing elaborate information on very early jobs. Unless an early part-time job had some unusual feature, there is little need to probe for likes, dislikes, and earnings. Rather, confine that discussion to such simple facts as duration of employment, number of hours worked, and reason for leaving.

With an older applicant who has a long job history, there is not sufficient time to obtain complete information on every experience. Moreover, older applicants probably haven't changed much in the last 10 years, but may be quite different from the way they were 15 or 20 years ago. This means that we move through early jobs quite rapidly and then give more exhaustive attention to recent experiences.

With Recent High School Graduates, Explore Summer Jobs Thoroughly

Many young applicants tend to skip over summer jobs too quickly, feeling that they are not relevant to the job for which they are applying. Summer jobs may not be entirely relevant, but they do tell us a great deal about applicants—the *initiative* they may have demonstrated in getting these jobs, the capacity to *adapt to and stay with boring or routine assignments, the ability to get along with people* from diverse backgrounds. Hence, when applicants tend to race over summer experiences, interviewers must use control with a comment such as, "I would like to know a lot more about that first summer job—how you got it, what you did, your likes, dislikes, and so forth."

EEO AREAS OF CONCERN

1. With those minorities or females where rapport seems more difficult to establish—and with such nonminorities as well—do not control quite as strictly. Permit such candidates to talk freely, even if the discourse tends to ramble and to be descriptive in nature. Although this will result in "more chaff along with the wheat" and will take more time, it will nevertheless provide more clues to behavior than would have come to light in an interview that was more strictly controlled.

2. With applicants who are particularly sensitive about the possibility that they may not be hired, interviewers should be especially adroit in the manner in which they interrupt such applicants for purposes of control. The timing and lubrication that are a part of interruption must be handled with great care. A sensitive person who feels that he or she has been cut off may interpret the cause of the interruption as a function of race, sex, or a handicap rather than as a function of completing the interview on time.

CHAPTER ELEVEN

Interpretation—
An Overview

In Chapter 7, we defined the two basic objectives of the interview as (1) developing relevant information and (2) interpreting information brought to light. In the three previous chapters, we have concentrated entirely on techniques designed to accomplish the first of these two objectives. Logically, then, the next three chapters are devoted to the task of assimilating all the employment information gathered and arriving at an employment decision.

Since interpretation is as complex as it is, this chapter is concerned with an overview of the subject—what interpretation involves and how to deal with it as an ongoing process. In Chapter 12 we discuss the *specifics* of exploring and interpreting the work history, and in Chapter 13 we apply the same treatment to the area of education.

FIRST CONSIDERATIONS

Since there is no point in interpreting information which we do not believe or cannot take at face value, we must first try to determine whether or not an applicant is telling the truth and whether or not the individual's standards are unrealistically high or low. Although answers to these two questions may not be obtained until the interview is perhaps half over, it seems logical to treat these two factors here before getting involved with interpretation per se.

How to Determine If an Applicant Is Telling the Truth

There are at least three valid means of determining the extent to which an applicant may be telling the truth: (1) *internal consistency*, (2) *the amount of unfavorable information an applicant provides*, and (3) *an obvious tendency to exaggerate accomplishments*.

By "internal consistency," we mean consistency of information between the two major areas of the interview, work history and education. Hence, if an individual is immature, evidence of this should appear in *both* of these major areas. It would be most unlikely, for example, that an applicant would reflect a high degree of maturity as a part of her or his work history but a low degree of maturity with respect to education. If such a situation should occur, we would immediately suspect that the person might not be telling the truth. To be more specific, a male applicant, for example, might reflect immaturity by mentioning unsound reasons for leaving jobs, poorly thought-out vocational goals, or aspirations way out of line with his abilities. In order for the discussion of education to be internally consistent, we might expect this same applicant to reveal such clues to immaturity as (1) studying hard on only those courses which he liked, (2) rationalizing failures by blaming teachers or the school system, or (3) selecting a major course of study with no thought at all as to how that major might be used after getting out of school. It is when the data become *inconsistent* that we begin to question the applicant's story. Thus, if the applicant cited above claimed that he (1) did his homework every single evening, (2) studied a lot harder on the courses that he did not like in order to get good grades, or (3) never cut any classes, we would begin to feel that he was telling us what he thought we wanted to hear rather than what actually happened.

When applicants appear to be leveling with us and providing us with a fair amount of unfavorable information along with the more favorable data, we regard this as firm evidence that they are telling the truth. If, for example, a female applicant admits that she was fired from a given job, that her attendance was not all that good, or that her typing speed is only 30 words a minute, we get the feeling that she is telling us her life story just as it actually occurred. With such an applicant, therefore, we can place considerable credence in statements about achievements.

Some applicants have a rather strong tendency to exaggerate their achievements, and this is quite easily picked up. In discussing outside interests, for example, a woman might claim that she reads four or five books a week. If that same woman had indicated a dislike of verbal subjects such as English, foreign languages, and history, her claim of reading four or five books a week would be internally inconsistent and probably an exaggeration. Likewise, a man who claims never to have spoken a word in anger strikes us as too good to be true and is probably exaggerating.

As we shall see later on in this chapter, however, we do not judge applicants' characteristics based on single clues. Rather, we try to develop a *series of clues* before making a judgment on a characteristic as important as, say, honesty. How we develop this kind of documentation is the subject of the three chapters on interpretation.

It may seem to some that no applicant would be likely to provide some of the negative information indicated above, but that is simply not true. When interviewers are successful in developing rapport and getting spontaneous information, they find themselves regularly obtaining information of a negative character that is even surprising to them.

Unrealistic Personal Standards

Even when we believe that applicants are telling the truth, we do not take all their comments at face value when we have determined that their personal standards are unrealistically high or low. When asked to tell about his shortcomings, a male applicant, for example, might indicate that he "probably should work a little harder." This might seem completely inconsistent if the interviewer has already developed a considerable amount of hard data supporting a willingness to work very hard. The interviewer may then suspect that the applicant's professed shortcoming stems from his tendency to be a perfectionist and hence to feel that he never does anything as well as he should. In such cases, interviewers rely upon accumulated hard data (clues to willingness to work hard picked up through the discussion of work history and education) rather than upon applicants' statements regarding their shortcomings. Personal standards may also indicate seeming inconsistencies at the other end of the spectrum. When asked to indicate her strengths, a woman, for example, may claim to be a hard worker when all the hard data indicate that just the opposite may be the case. But the inconsistency here may be based upon *low personal standards* rather than upon dishonesty. Some people's standards are so low that it does not take much to satisfy them. Hence, they may think of themselves as hard workers when this is actually not the case at all.

Fortunately, the hard data (clues to behavior) usually turn out to be consistent with an applicant's own assessment of his or her abilities. It is easy to believe an applicant's claim to being a hard worker when we have already noted such factors as spending long hours on a variety of jobs, carrying out as many as two or three jobs simultaneously, or putting in a full summer of extremely hard manual work such as unloading boxcars. Inconsistencies that are due to unrealistically high or low personal standards will not be frequent, but they should be identified as such when they do occur.

PROCESS OF INTERPRETATION

As one might expect, it is easier to train interviewers to secure the necessary information than it is to train them to interpret the findings. The information-getting techniques discussed in earlier chapters work so well that, within 2 or 3 days, even novices can learn to apply them effectively so that they usually experience little difficulty in getting candidates to open up. But learning to interpret is an entirely different matter.

Since interpretation obviously involves a mental process, it requires a fair amount of analytical ability—ability not only to recognize clues to behavior but to catalog such clues in terms of assets and shortcomings. A good interview produces a large mass of information *only part of which is relevant in terms of interpretation.* As the discussion progresses, the interviewer must constantly separate the wheat from the chaff, searching for clues to such characteristics as willingness to work, ability to get along with others, emotional maturity, and leadership potential.

Interpretation As an Ongoing Process

Interviewers who wait until the end of the interview to decide what they think of an applicant are hopelessly lost. The interpretation process, in fact, begins as soon as applicants enter the room and continues until they leave. Clues to behavior build throughout the interview so that an applicant's overall qualifications normally become quite evident by the time the interview has been concluded. Interviewers who do a good *ongoing* job of interpretation should know whether or not they want to hire the individual by the time that person leaves the room. This may not necessarily be possible during the early part of an interviewer's training, but as the trainee interviews more and more people, he or she will find it increasingly easy to catalog clues to behavior and to arrive at employment decisions earlier. In interviewing more and more people, moreover, interviewers build up a *frame of reference* which enables them to compare the qualifications of a given applicant with those of all the other people they have recently seen.

Interviewers Learn to Mask Their Reactions

As the applicant's story unfolds, interviewers mentally scrutinize each bit of information for possible clues to behavior. Yet they carry out this evaluation process in such a way that they completely mask their true reaction and hence do not give the applicant the slightest inkling of how they are interpreting a remark. To do otherwise might risk loss of rapport. An interviewer who registers surprise or disapproval as a result of uncovering unfavorable information frequently turns applicants off to the point where the interviewer never succeeds in getting them to open up again.

Cataloging Clues

As soon as an applicant enters the room, interviewers should begin to get impressions of that individual in terms of possible effectiveness in the job for which he or she is being considered. It may be noted, for example, that a candidate presents a nice appearance and has an appreciable amount of poise and presence—clues that may be cataloged mentally as factors in the person's possible effectiveness with people. As the interview progresses, the interviewer may become impressed with the complete candor with which the applicant discusses strengths and shortcomings and may catalog that as an indication of sincerity and maturity. (Individuals who know themselves in terms of their strengths and limitations are often more mature than their chronological age group.) Later on, the candidate may indicate that he or she often stays on after quitting time in order to get a job done or even comes in on a Saturday. The interviewer catalogs this, naturally, as a clue to conscientiousness and willingness to work. And so it goes throughout the interview. Each statement the applicant makes is carefully examined in terms of its implied as well as its obvious meaning. Resulting clues to behavior are then mentally cataloged as possible indications of such traits as willingness to work hard, emotional maturity, adaptability, ability to get along with people, and leadership potential.

Relevance of Applicant's Work History and Education

Interviewers look not only for clues to behavior but also for the extent to which an applicant's previous experience and training have provided adequate preparation for the position in question. If the job in question, for example, involves shift work, interviewers would be quick to note any previous shift-work experience and how the individual reacted to this. They know full well that individuals who have already experienced shift work know what they're getting into and adapt to it much more readily than someone without such experience. This is not to say that applicants without shift-work experience would necessarily be rejected. It simply means that those who have had this experience, other things being equal, would receive more favorable consideration.

Mentally Organize a List of Assets and Liabilities

As the discussion progresses, interviewers mentally compile a list of the applicant's strengths and shortcomings with respect to the job under consideration. Although their outward manner is permissive and disarming, they nevertheless evaluate analytically and critically everything an applicant has to say. As the interview progresses from work history to education and finally to outside interests, a general pattern of behavior normally begins to make itself evident. Thus, interviewers may get clue after clue attesting to a candidate's forcefulness, willingness to accept responsibility, and strong drive to get things done quickly. At the same time, since a high degree of strength in certain areas may be accompanied by concomitant shortcomings in other areas, interviewers may also pick up a series of clues indicating lack of tact, inflexibility, or even ruthlessness. As they catalog such clues, they find it increasingly possible to build a list of assets and liabilities. In fact, such a list of assets and liabilities should be so well documented by the end of the discussion that interviewers can write them out immediately after the applicant leaves the room. At that point, interviewers make the hiring decision on the basis of the extent to which the assets outweigh the liabilities or vice versa.

Searching for Clues to Mental Capacity

In addition to our search for personality traits and relevance of previous experience and training; we also look for the *level of the applicant's basic abilities.* As noted in Chapter 6, aptitude tests can be of tremendous help in establishing the level of a candidate's mental, verbal, and numerical ability, clerical aptitude, and mechanical comprehension. However, such test results are not always available, and in such cases interviewers must do the best they can to establish ability levels on the basis of interviewer findings. Specific suggestions for accomplishing this task will be found in subsequent chapters. Suffice it to say here, though, that some of the best clues to mental ability will be found in such factors as (1) level of grades in terms of effort required to get those grades, (2) college board scores, if applicable, and (3) an applicant's ability to respond to the more difficult depth questions.

WHAT TO INTERPRET

As indicated earlier, every interview results in *relevant* and *irrelevant* information. Actually, much of what the applicant may have to say is likely to be *descriptive*, providing little in the way of clues to behavior. Interviewers, of course, try to keep such information to a minimum, controlling the discussion so that applicants concentrate on evaluative data. Even so, a certain amount of descriptive information is certain to ensue. Interviewers naturally pay as little attention as possible to such irrelevant data, constantly identifying the important information and making their interpretations accordingly.

In general, the more relevant information is likely to be found in applicants' *attitudes* and *reactions*. Thus, we learn much more about people as a result of their attitudes and reactions toward a given job than we do from a description of the job duties. Such attitudes and reactions often provide specific clues to such important factors as emotional maturity, willingness to work hard, tact, and self-confidence.

Since we are also looking for the relevance of applicants' work experience and education in terms of the job for which they are being considered, we must carry a mental picture of the job and worker specifications into the discussion with us. As we listen to the description of previous jobs, for example, we must be quick to notice any similarity between those jobs and the job for which the applicant is being considered. We must also decide whether candidates are capable of performing the job in question with minimum orientation or whether a protracted training period will be necessary to bring them to a productive level. In like manner, we evaluate candidates' education, deciding whether or not they have the kind and quality of technical training that will enable them to perform effectively.

HOW TO INTERPRET

We have talked above about the importance of determining the *relevance* of an applicant's work history and education. This is a relatively simple task since one has only to compare what candidates have done in the past with what they may be expected to do on the job for which they are being considered. All that is required is an ability to get information and a clear picture of the demands of the job in question. Understanding and utilizing the process described below—the concept of *contrast*—will help immeasurably in carrying out this interpretative function.

Concept of Contrast

This process involves the continual contrasting of each aspect of an applicant's job and school history with the specifications of the job under consideration. In those areas where little or no contrast is involved—or where the difference is in a positive direction—no real adjustment problem exists. This of course represents a favorable finding. On the other hand, where the contrast is appreciable, candidates might be expected to experience a very real adjustment problem in acclimating to the new job situation. Although the difference may be insufficient to exclude applicants from further consideration, such a difference nevertheless represents an unfavorable factor.

Let us assume, for example, that a given job calls for shift work and weekend work. Applicants who have done shift work and weekend work as a part of their previous experience—and who have apparently been able to accept it quite readily as part of the job—might be expected to be able to adjust to the new job much more easily than applicants without such experience. With the former group the contrast would not appear to be very great, while with the latter group the contrast would in all likelihood be significant.

We would find another such unfavorable contrast in applicants who are already earning more money on their present job than what they would be paid as a starting salary on the new job. They might express a willingness to take the new job at a lower salary because it may offer greater long-range opportunity. Once they have been on the job for a while, however, a certain amount of dissatisfaction is likely to develop. This dissatisfaction may be stimulated further by a spouse who finds it necessary to make ends meet on a smaller budget. Many such individuals decide that they can't wait for future salary increases and begin looking for another job. If, on the other hand, applicants are to be paid a starting salary in excess of their present earnings, they can be expected to be more satisfied with their new lot, other things being equal. This of course represents a difference, or contrast, in the positive direction and is evaluated by the interviewer as a *favorable factor*.

The kind of close supervision involved in previous jobs and in a proposed new assignment may also provide an unfavorable contrast. A secretary who has had previous experience running an office and taking care of much of the correspondence might become quickly dissatisfied in a new job where every single piece of correspondence was dictated and where everything was very closely supervised. When such individuals take new positions involving much closer supervision and much less opportunity to exercise their own initiative, they normally find adjustment somewhat difficult. The alert interviewer recognizes the potentially unfavorable contrast and adds this to the list of negative factors.

Interpretation by Direct Observation

One can make *some* valid judgments about people simply by observing them directly. Thus, interviewers find it quite easy to evaluate such obvious characteristics as appearance, poise, presence, grooming, and self-expression. They simply observe an applicant's outward behavior during the discussion and make their judgments on these characteristics accordingly.

It is even possible to learn something about personal forcefulness and tact by means of direct observation. For example, the interviewer might note that a given candidate's personality has considerable impact and that the individual is exceedingly forceful and dynamic in conversation. Since personal forcefulness is an element of leadership, the interviewer would be quick to note that as a favorable factor. However, that same individual may frequently interrupt an interviewer in the middle of a sentence or may talk disparagingly about certain minority groups without knowing whether or not the interviewer may be a member of such groups. This kind of behavior obviously represents a lack of tact and social sensitivity.

It must be pointed out again, though, that interpretation by direct observation is limited to the more obvious or easy-to-evaluate characteristics. It is of very little use in determining the more important factors such as willingness to work, emotional maturity, intelligence, and perseverance. Yet, interpretation by direct observations is the only means available to most untrained interviewers. This is why the interview has often fared so poorly when subjected to validation studies.

Interpretation by Inference

Since interpretation by direct observation represents a relatively limited device, what method do we use to evaluate the more important characteristics? We use a time-tested method called *interpretation by inference*. By definition, this means that we *infer* from a *series of clues* the extent to which an individual possesses a given trait or ability. The phrase "series of clues" in this definition is extremely important since it would be most unfair and inaccurate to base an evaluation on a single unfavorable situation. Even if a person admits to having been fired from a given job, that, in itself, would not represent an adequate basis for assuming the person was a troublemaker or a poor worker. It is conceivable, in fact, that the supervisor may have been at fault. But, if there are problems on other jobs, if the person talks disparagingly about coworkers, and if there were disciplinary problems in school, we can determine with some assurance that this individual is not able to get along with people very well. This assurance stems from the fact that we have developed a *series* of clues rather than based our evaluation on a single happenstance. And, because these clues have spanned two areas of the interview—work history and education—we have established a pattern of internal consistency. When an individual has any given trait in some abundance, clues to such a trait will not be limited to a single area of the interview. Rather, such clues will surface in both the work history and education.

In our efforts to document a trait such as immaturity, clues to this important shortcoming might surface in the work history as poor judgment in leaving certain jobs and unwillingness to make current sacrifices for future gains, or as aspirations which are quite out of line with the individual's abilities. Clues to this same shortcoming could conceivably come to light in the educational area in the form of rationalizing failures—blaming poor grades on the teachers or schools. Clues of a similar nature might be identified in a failure to study for subjects which the person did not like or in poor judgment in selecting a major course of study.

In evaluating older individuals, persons in their early forties for example, we must be very careful not to evaluate them in terms of *what they were like 15 or 20 years ago*. A young man, for example, in his early twenties may have been quite footloose and fancy-free, hopping from one job to another without any sense of direction at all, but that same individual may have settled down to the point that his history over the past 10 years or so may have been very stable. Hence, we base our evaluation on clues to behavior based on the person's more recent history.

We have indicated earlier that clues must be interpreted as soon as they become evident. This provides interviewers with a beginning or starting point on which they can build later on. Using such a clue as a *temporary* supposition, they mentally catalog it as a possible indication of a given trait. With this supposition as a foundation, they subsequently probe at appropriate intervals through-

out the discussion for additional specific clues to support the supposition. In the case cited above, an interviewer would have got-
ten an early clue to immaturity, thus providing a temporary
supposition; however, since clues to immaturity were not evident
in the man's history for the 10 most recent years, the interviewer
would have had to throw out the initial hypothesis. On the other
hand, some people never seem to grow up. Evidence may show
that job-hopping, chronic dissatisfaction with practically every
job, and poor judgment are still deeply rooted in an individual's
behavior. In such a case, we have ample evidence—in the form of
many clues pointing in the same direction—to eliminate the candidate from further consideration.

For purposes of further illustration, let us assume that an applicant has expressed a strong dislike for detail in connection with a
prior clerical job. The interviewer catalogs this appropriately and
wisely decides to wait, listen, and not *prejudge*, at the same time,
actively probing for further evidence, particularly in those areas
which would be most likely to provide clues to a dislike of detail.
Thus, when the applicant discusses a subsequent job as a computer
programmer, the interviewer, knowing that this type of work
involves a great amount of detail, will try to get further evidence
of this trait by stimulating in the applicant a spontaneous recital
of likes and dislikes in that job. If the individual does not mention
attention to detail as either a like or a dislike, the interviewer may
ask a question specifically about the applicant's feelings concerning the detail involved. Later on, the interviewer may probe in
like manner for the candidate's reaction to a detail-oriented subject in school such as mechanical drawing and toward the end of
the discussion may try to get further confirmation of a possible
dislike of and inability to carry out detailed work by bringing this
up under self-evaluation as a possible shortcoming. Utilizing the
double-edged question, the interviewer might say, "What about
attention to detail? Do you have as much of this as you would like
to have, or is this something that you could improve a little bit?"
If, at that point, the applicant candidly admits to not handling
detail well, the interviewer will have brought to light a serious
shortcoming, *providing that the worker specifications indicate
attention to detail as an important requisite.*

We therefore see that interpretation by inference goes on
throughout the interview, the interviewer making tentative hypo-

theses and probing specifically for confirming evidence. Remember, too, that interviewers are charged with the responsibility of developing clues to a *variety* of characteristics. They are therefore confronted with a mentally demanding assignment. This is the primary reason why they must be so skilled in the mechanics of the interview that these become almost second nature. Once this level has been achieved in the sense that interviewers do not have to concern themselves about mechanics anymore, they automatically become better *listeners* and can devote the major portion of their attention to the process of evaluation.

Hypotheses Based on Leads from Previous Selection Steps

Since the interview is preceded by such employment steps as the application form, the preliminary interview, and the aptitude tests, it represents an ideal opportunity to follow up on some of the *leads* which may have emerged from some of those early steps. Such leads often give the interviewer a tremendous head start as far as the interpretive process is concerned. Even before the interview begins, for example, the interviewer may have a lead to possible lack of motivation. Let us assume that the tests of mental ability reflect a high level of intelligence. The interviewer will expect to see this reflected in above-average grades in school. If such does not turn out to be the case, the interviewer will immediately probe for reasons why, suspecting low-level application or disorganized study habits. Or, in another example, the preliminary interviewer may have noted a slight tendency to be evasive. With that lead in mind, the final interviewer will be immediately alerted for any signs of dishonesty. Thus, by studying information available to them before the interview, interviewers can frequently develop usable hypotheses which they carry into the discussion and seek to support or reject on the basis of the evidence presented. It should be emphasized, though, that a lead is just that and nothing more. If it cannot be supported by hard data, it must be discarded.

CHAPTER TWELVE

Interpreting Work History

In the previous chapter, we talked about general factors of interpretation—what the process involves and how to go about putting it into operation. In this chapter, we get down to *specifics;* we consider what the discussion of work history may be able to tell us about an applicant's personality, motivation, and abilities. In addition to establishing the relevance of applicants' previous work experience in terms of the job for which they are being considered, we need to look specifically for clues to such factors as mental capacity (if tests are not available), honesty, adaptability, and other work-related personality traits.

We have mentioned earlier that this kind of interview differs from most interviews in the sense that we try to *document* our findings with hard data. Instead of coming away from an interview with a hunch that a given individual may be a hard worker, we search for data to support such a finding, in the form of such factors as long hours spent on a given job without complaint, substantial numbers of hours a week working on a part-time job while carrying a full academic load, or perseverance on a summer job involving hard manual work for the complete summer. In our attempts to get hard data, moreover, we make every attempt to *quantify* information—to get numbers. When a person works on a part-time job while attending school, for example, we need to get the number of hours worked per week. It might be as few as 6 or 8 or as many as 25 to 30. By the same token, we are not satisfied when people tell us that their attendance record was "good." Employees' ideas of good attendance can vary greatly. We try to get quantification by asking the number of days absent during the year.

Applicants' work history ordinarily represents a major portion of their life's experience and, as such, not only provides an indication of their ability to do a certain job in question but also supplies many clues as to *how* they will do it. The manner in which a person works is often the best single source of information concerning personality strengths and weaknesses. It is fitting, then, that applicants be encouraged to give a rather exhaustive account of their work background, particularly as it pertains to items listed under work experience on the interview guide.

In this chapter, we will offer suggestions for structuring discussion of the work history. This will be followed by an item-by-item discussion of factors listed under work experience on the interview guide.

HOW TO STRUCTURE DISCUSSION OF THE WORK HISTORY

The reader will recall that, in our efforts to get applicants talking spontaneously, we begin the discussion of all major areas of the interview with a comprehensive lead question. In launching the work history discussion, interviewers may use such a comprehensive question as, "Suppose you start by telling me about your work experience, beginning with the first job and working up to the present. I would like to know how you got each job, what you did, your likes, dislikes, earnings, and so forth. Where do we start? Did you have any jobs while attending high school?" In talking about various jobs, applicants will normally provide spontaneous information concerning many of the factors listed under work history on the interview guide. When they fail to provide such information—or if they do not discuss important factors in sufficient detail

—interviewers should prompt them by adroitly worded follow-up questions and comments.

Remember, too, that we try to keep the work history pure, in the sense that we encourage applicants to concentrate on *jobs*, without supplying much information about other interview areas. When applicants begin to ramble or to provide too much descriptive information, we try to control the interview by adroitly interrupting them with a carefully timed compliment and bringing them back to the subject under discussion.

Military service should be discussed at the point at which it occurs chronologically in the individual's work history and should be treated just like any other important job. Thus, in the case of a man who went into the Army after completing high school, we would discuss the jobs he had while in high school and then launch into a thorough discussion of his Army experience. This would be followed by a discussion of jobs he may have had after getting out of the Army. In order to avoid spending too much time on the military experience, take individuals quickly through their various assignments. Then ask about their overall likes and dislikes about the military experience as a whole, rather than getting reactions to every assignment. Look for relationships with superiors and associates, any leadership experience, and specific skills (and/or training) which may be relevant to the job for which they are being considered. Since the military experience often represents a period of appreciable individual growth and development, it is usually beneficial to ask a question such as, "In what ways do you think your military experience changed you? What specific traits or abilities do you think you developed during that time?"

A discussion of each of the factors listed under work history on the interview guide follows in this chapter. Each factor is treated in some detail, in terms of both how to get the information and how to interpret the resulting data.

RELEVANCE OF PRIOR JOBS

Other things being equal, job relevance plays an important part in deciding the extent to which applicants may be qualified for a given job. The fewer *adjustments and adaptations* individuals have to make in moving from previous jobs to a new job, the more likely they are to find the new job satisfying, and the more quickly they should be able to reach a satisfactory rate of production. If, in undertaking a new assignment, individuals are asked to perform operations under environmental conditions they have grown used to on previous jobs, they usually find it possible to adapt to the new job quite comfortably and quickly. On the other hand, if everything is completely new to them, they often suffer a certain amount of "culture shock," in the sense that they find so many new things to learn and to get used to that they initially have great difficulty getting organized and concentrating on what is expected of them.

As an applicant relates her or his job history, the interviewer mentally checks this experience against worker specifications of the job under consideration. If the applicant has indicated no job choice, the interviewer makes a mental comparison of the general similarity of the individual's work experience to the worker specifications which that experience most closely approximates. Before the interview is terminated, both interviewer and interviewee must have agreed on the specific job for which the applicant seems best-qualified.

Essentially, evaluation of work experience involves an investigation of three simple questions:

1. What did the applicant do?
2. How did he or she do it?
3. What did he or she do it with?

Items listed on the interview guide will provide appreciable help in securing answers to these basic questions. These items are discussed here in the same order in which they appear on the interview guide.

Similar Job Duties?

In evaluating candidates for plant or office jobs, it is important to know exactly what individuals did on their previous jobs. In a plant job, did they lay out their own work, set up their machines, and check their own work for accuracy, or did they simply operate the machine, leaving setup to a setup person and checking of accuracy to an inspector? In like manner, when evaluating the work of a stenographer, it would be important to know whether his or her duties were limited to taking dictation and typing or included independent handling of some correspondence not requiring a dictated reply.

In determining suitability for most jobs, it is often unnecessary to find someone who has performed exactly the same job duties. Rather, the interviewer evaluates the general nature of candidates' experience, assuming that they should be able to carry out new duties that are generally similar to what they have done in the past. Individuals who have made satisfactory scores on tests of hand and finger dexterity, for example, should be able to handle a *variety* of assembly operations. Hence, a new type of assembly operation should not prove much of a problem if they have already done some type of assembly work in the past.

Any Experience Working Shifts or Weekends?

Persons who have been conditioned to working shifts and weekends usually find little difficulty in making the transition to a new job involving these working conditions, but people without this prior conditioning often find adjustment difficult indeed. Working shifts and weekends involves such a different lifestyle that people in many European countries, for example, have simply refused to embrace it at all, and most workers in this country would probably prefer not to work on shifts if they had any choice in the matter. Hence, there must be some powerful incentive—usually in the form of substantially higher wages than they have previously earned—to attract them to a job involving shift work when they have never done this before. Fortunately, the human organism is highly malleable and can adapt to a wide variety of difficult situations *if necessary*. (People fighting under conditions of modern warfare represents a case in point.)

We all know that both men and women can adjust to shift work and even weekend work if the incentive is high enough. Even so, this involves a relatively high degree of *adaptability* on their part, so adaptability is an important trait for which interviewers must search—particularly in those individuals for whom the new job will involve a major change in lifestyle. Adaptability can best be assessed by noting the extent to which individuals have been able to make adjustments to new and changing situations in the past, with respect to both work history and education.

Experience with Required Hand or Machine Tools?

Good interviewers will know enough about the standard makes of machine tools to be able to inquire intelligently of persons claiming experience on a particular machine. They can ask them to identify and tell the functions of various parts of the machine, discussing cutting tools, speeds, feeds, and the like. Applicants for clerical work, moreover, can be questioned about proficiency in using a variety of office machines, including computers and word processors. It is a matter of some interest that many clerical people dislike typing information from dictaphone machines. Since this type of dictation is gaining wide utilization in industry today, interviewers must make a special point of raising this question with people being considered for a job of this sort.

In hiring women for jobs requiring the use of hand tools, it is very important to find out whether they have ever had occasion to use such tools in any capacity. Many women have never used hand tools to an appreciable extent and may find this one of the most difficult phases of the job to master. While keeping this in mind, interviewers should not pursue such information any less rigorously for male applicants. Anyone familiar with the use of tools, other things being equal, can be expected to reach a standard rate of production in a considerably shorter period of time than someone without such familiarity—where, of course, the job requires frequent use of hand tools.

Similar Working Conditions?

As applicants discuss their work history, from earlier jobs to the more recent experiences, interviewers should mentally note the extent to which they have had an opportunity to become conditioned to the type of working conditions to which they will be subjected on a new job. Thus, where the job to be filled has disagreeable features, it is worthwhile to find out whether applicants have grown used to these conditions on earlier jobs. Have they become accustomed to standing all day, working in excessive oil and dirt, working under artificial light? Have they become conditioned to the noise of a factory? Are they in the habit of working in a situation where unpleasant odors or extreme variations in temperature are a factor? Are they familiar with safety practices essential to the performance of the job? Have they ever been exposed to similar occupational hazards?

A hand trucker who has always worked inside sometimes has difficulty when assigned to outside platform work because of the change in weather conditions. Someone with considerable experience working in a library might find the noise of a riveting operation so distracting that adjustment to such a job might be almost impossible. The noise level in some factory operations is incredibly high. As indicated earlier, interviewers should visit such operations with a view to understanding the kind of environmental conditions to which new workers are to be subjected.

Determining the degree of supervision in former jobs often reveals that so much adjustment would have to be made in undertaking the job in question that successful performance might not reasonably be assured. Have the candidates been used to working on their own, laying out their own work and making many of the decisions that have to be made in the performance of their jobs? Or have they always been closely supervised, in the sense that most of their work has been planned for them and most decisions referred to their boss? A good illustration of the former is the plant pickup truck driver whose work occurs out of the plant. The driver contacts superiors only two or three times a day, making the decisions as to the order of calls and planning lunch periods without supervision. The plumber's helper, on the other hand, works entirely under the direction of the plumber to whom he or she has been assigned. Leaving practically nothing to the helper's judgment, the plumber lays out the work, specifying, for example, the size of the pipe to be used, the length to be cut, the type of thread dye needed, and the number of inches of thread required.

Candidates who have had pretty much of a free hand in handling their previous job assignments would be expected to have great difficulty adjusting to a job where they would be closely supervised. By the same token, many persons who have grown accustomed to being closely supervised on previous jobs might be like a "fish out of water" in a job where they were required to exercise initiative and make their own decisions. Many such individuals simply would not have sufficient self-confidence to operate successfully in this situation.

Where a job involves considerable attention to detail, accuracy, thoroughness, and "number crunching," many applicants would not be able to handle such confinement. In general, work of a highly detailed nature is better-handled by persons who tend to be somewhat introverted. Out-and-out extroverts would become distracted in such confining jobs as drafting, filing, and computer programming.

Many entry-level plant and office jobs involve an appreciable amount of routine. This, of course, is particularly true of many types of assembly operations. In such jobs, workers perform the same operations over and over again all day long. In selecting people for such jobs, therefore, one should look for individuals who have performed this type of routine work in other job situations and who apparently have grown accustomed to it. It should be noted in passing that the brighter the individual is, the more likely he or she is to become quickly fed up with a routine assignment. Quite understandably, brighter people are happier in jobs that involve some judgment and some opportunity to utilize their imagination. Interviewers would only be justified in hiring bright people for routine jobs, therefore, when those jobs represented a relatively short first step to something more demanding. Most bright people are quite willing to put up with a dull job if they know they can look forward to something much more challenging within the near future.

What About Applicants with Limited Plant or Office Experience?

Women without industrial experience are moving into the labor market in ever-increasing numbers. Just because they have no relevant plant or office experience is not in itself justification for rejecting them. Rather, in the spirit of affirmative action, ways must be found to place them in jobs where they would be most likely to succeed. Even so, interviewers have the responsibility to look beyond the "average" homemaker without experience to those who can be evaluated as *best-qualified*. Women who fulfill the requirements of the three M's (mental ability, motivation, and maturity) and who are also *adaptable* can learn to adjust to a great variety of factory and office job situations and in most, if not all, cases can eventually handle these jobs as well as their male counterparts.

Homemakers may have had early jobs (before marriage) which

may provide some clues to their behavior, and, as will be noted in Chapter 13, their outside interests may provide additional hard data concerning their abilities and personality traits. The experience of running community drives, chairing committees, serving as club officers, and handling other positions of responsibility outside of the home has a tendency to prepare the individual for taking on new experiences in industry. When, in addition to the demanding job of rearing children and maintaining a household, a person is able to take on any kind of an outside job, that individual can certainly be classified as having energy, stamina, and a willingness to work.

Interviewers face the same problem with recent high school graduates, few of whom have had experience at all relevant to jobs for which they may be applying in industry. The problem of assessing the individual's ability for success in untried fields is even greater here than in the case of the inexperienced homemaker. Recent high school graduates are *younger* and, therefore, have fewer experiences of any kind to evaluate. With such individuals, interviewers must concentrate on summer jobs and clues that can be picked up from the academic experience in high school. The best-qualified high school graduates will have shown initiative in getting summer jobs, and many will have handled their first job so well that they are invited back for a second summer. As will be noted in the next chapter, they also will have demonstrated such important factors as diligence, intelligence, and sociability in the manner in which they have handled their high school studies and extracurricular affairs.

LIKES

As the applicant proceeds from job to job during the interview, it is advisable to repeat part of the lead question: *"Tell me about the next job—how you got it, what you did, your likes, dislikes, earnings, and so forth."* Such a question obviates many questions such as: "What did you like?" "What didn't you like so well?" "What were your earnings?" When interviewers develop sufficient rapport, they get much of this information *spontaneously.* Even so, the subject of what individuals *liked* about their various jobs is so important that a fair amount of concentration in this area is quite justified. When an applicant does not mention likes at all, a question such as, "What were *some* of the things you liked best on that job?" is very useful. The injection of the word "some" indicates that the interviewer expects more than a single like. In discussing important jobs or jobs held for a fair amount of time, interviewers should probe for more than a single like. They should say, "What else did you find satisfying in that job?"

Experience has shown—and it is entirely reasonable—that people tend to perform best on those tasks which they like. Ideally, then, the most favorable situation develops when applicants' likes on previous jobs correspond with important elements of jobs for which they are being considered. If they have previously shown a liking for detail and have demonstrated thoroughness and accuracy, for example, they should have little difficulty adjusting to a new job involving such detail. People who liked working with their hands in their previous jobs—and whose aptitude tests show good hand and finger dexterity—should have little difficulty adjusting to a new job involving a variety of hand operations.

Likes on previous jobs can, of course, supply many clues to abilities, personality traits, and motivation. This is why it is often more rewarding to spend time on reactions (likes and dislikes) to a job rather than on a description of the duties of the job. Persons who have always enjoyed the people that they worked with on previous jobs are, more often than not, individuals who have the ability to get along with others. People who do not mind staying late at night occasionally because they enjoy getting a job done are often highly motivated individuals.

Likes are equally valuable in providing clues to possible shortcomings. The applicant who liked a job because of its regular hours, frequent vacations, and lack of overtime work may be the kind of person who does not like to put in extra effort on a job. If suspicion of this trait can be supported by subsequent clues pointing in the same direction, the interviewer will have come up with an important finding concerning the person's lack of motivation. A person who greatly enjoyed a job because it provided a "high degree of freedom" may be reflecting on the one hand, a desire for responsibility but, on the other hand, a tendency to be overly independent. In response to such a finding, then, the interviewer would do some two-step probing in order to find out what there was about having a completely free hand that gave the individual so much satisfaction.

DISLIKES

Once applicants have had a chance to discuss their likes, they are normally quite willing to talk about their dislikes, particularly if good rapport has been established. At the same time, interviewers should approach this subject adroitly by softening their follow-up question. Instead of asking about a person's dislikes, they should pose such a question as, "What were some of the things you found less satisfying on that job?" It is possible that an applicant may not have had any actual job dislikes in a particular situation; however, considered relatively, there are always some aspects of a job that are less satisfying than others. Many times applicants may bring up dislikes on their own. In such cases, it is possible that the dislikes are more deeply felt, and, hence, they may be more meaningful.

As in the case of likes, dislikes often provide clues to personality, motivation, and character. The college student who "had nothing in common" with coworkers on a summer job may be lacking in *common touch*, an important ingredient in one's ability to get along with others. The applicant who expresses dislike for a previous job "because it was too messy" would not be expected to like work of a similar nature in a new assignment. People who complain about "the drudgery of detail" on previous assignments, of course, are not likely to adjust easily to new jobs with detail orientation. Applicants who complain about being left on their own much of the time without much direction may be providing clues to lack of confidence and overdependence upon others. Other applicants who complain that "The job was too complicated. There were too many things to think of at once," may be providing clues to lack of flexibility or perhaps to some mental limitation. In any event, such clues are only "straws in the wind" until they have been confirmed by subsequent clues pointing in the same direction. Even so, they provide valuable hypotheses. We should not leave the subject of dislikes without pointing out that some job dislikes can also reveal clues to assets. In fact, willingness to talk about dislikes frequently provides clues to honesty, sincerity, and even self-confidence. When an applicant discusses negative information candidly and objectively, the interviewer will likely conclude that he or she is getting the complete story and, hence, give the person credit for being honest and sincere. Similarly, a dislike of the routine nature of a previous job may point to the fact that a person is bright and, hence, cut out for better things.

CONDITIONING TO WORK

People who have become conditioned to hard work and long hours in the past can be expected to apply themselves with like diligence in the future. When a person works 50 or 60 hours a week over a protracted period of time, he or she develops an *increased capacity for constructive effort.* This is equally true of people who carry out a full-time job during the day and go to school at night. Some individuals actually go to school 3 nights a week, after working full-time during the day. In so doing, they become accustomed or conditioned to spending long hours on constructive efforts. When such individuals complete their night-school work or terminate their extended hours on a job and return to a normal 8-hour day, they are usually able to apply themselves much more vigorously than the average individual. Boys and girls brought up on a farm are also normally conditioned to hard work. In addition to their schoolwork, they have to do their chores before and after school. Such chores often consist of heavy manual work such as getting in hay, cleaning stalls, feeding stock, and even helping with the milking. Any activity of this kind that has extended one's capacity for hard work represents a valuable asset.

EARNINGS (STARTING AND ENDING)

Even though this information has been requested on the application form, it is important to go over it again in the interview. For one thing, we like to see if earnings information provided in the interview checks with application information, thereby bringing to light clues to honesty or perhaps lack of it. Secondly, by tone of voice and facial expressions, applicants often unconsciously indicate satisfaction with their earnings, or perhaps dissatisfaction. When applicants indicate satisfaction with earnings which are below average for the kind of work they did, they put a price tag on what they think of their own abilities and this indirectly may reflect lack of self-confidence.

The pattern of earnings over the years represents one important criterion of an individual's job progress to date. In cases where there has been steady earnings progress, it can usually be assumed that such individuals are persons of some ability. The indications are that their supervisors thought well of them. In such cases, it is a good idea to probe deeper with a question such as, "What traits or abilities do you think you demonstrated on that job that influenced your supervisors to raise your salary to the extent that they did?" Answers to this question often come in the form of, "I guess they thought I worked harder than many of the other people. I think they also realized that I am reliable, I seldom missed a day of work, and I was almost always on time."

When ending earnings are higher than beginning earnings—as we would hope they would be—it is beneficial to ask whether increases were merit increases or general increases won by a union. Merit increases are almost always significant, since they usually indicate that an individual was a good worker.

Lack of salary progress frequently reflects significant shortcomings. A man, for example, in his middle thirties who has shown relatively little salary progress in the last 10 years is usually one who is lacking in ability, reliability, effectiveness of personality, or motivation. Of course, there may have been factors outside his control. He may have been unwilling to give up the security of a particular job because of the serious illness of a member of his family. In order to probe further for his reactions to low earnings, an interviewer might say, "How do you *feel about* your salary? Are you relatively satisfied with what you are making, or do you think that your job merits something more?" The subsequent response may indicate a number of interesting clues to behavior, including lack of salary aspirations, bitterness over lack of salary progress, rationalization of the situation, or general recognition of shortcomings and willingness to accept his lot in life.

When evaluating applicants for a new job, interviewers should give particular attention to the relationship between earnings on the last job and the starting salary on the job for which they are being considered. As discussed earlier, if they have already earned appreciably more than the new job pays, serious dissatisfaction is likely to develop later on. At the time of the interview, they may profess a willingness to take the new job because of its greater responsibilities. Once on that job, however, they will normally become relatively unhappy—at least until such time as their salary equals their previous earnings.

When the salary of the new job is substantially higher than an individual has ever earned before, the interviewer naturally suspects that the person's earnings have failed to keep pace with his or her years of experience and probes for the underlying reasons. Nevertheless, higher starting salaries on a new job relative to what an individual has earned previously represent a positive factor. It is only natural to expect the person to be more satisfied with higher earnings and to work harder and be more appreciative of the new position.

It is often helpful to ask an applicant to discuss the wage payment or wage incentive plan which was in effect during prior employment at a particular company. This prepares the way for further questions about (1) starting salary, (2) peak earnings, and (3) earnings at the time of leaving the company. If separation earnings are less than peak earnings, there must be a reason. Try to find out whether this is a normal condition of the job or whether it represents a demotion.

REASONS FOR CHANGING JOBS

Since some applicants are sensitive about their reasons for leaving certain jobs, this topic must be approached with some delicacy. The subject can be probed indirectly by asking about additional dislikes. A simple question such as, "What were some of the other things you found less satisfying on that job?" frequently results in a spontaneous discussion regarding reasons for leaving. An applicant might say, "Well, I guess the job was just too monotonous—so monotonous that I became fed up and decided to leave." When indirect questioning does not produce the desired results, interviewers have to become more direct by saying, *"How did you happen to* leave that job?"

Here again, the way in which the person responds is almost as important as the reasons themselves. Any tendency to explain away failure to adjust to the job should be regarded with suspicion. A trained interviewer can tactfully explore such areas further and frequently come up with the real reason why the individual left the job. The following represents a suggested means of investigating this situation: "Your next job doesn't seem to represent very much improvement in either wages or opportunity. Why did you make the change? You can be frank with me, you know." This approach may eventually reveal that one or more of the reasons listed below played a large part in causing termination of the job:

1. Incompetence on a particular job
2. Quick temper
3. Inflexibility
4. Wanderlust
5. Poor personal habits
6. Friction with supervisors
7. Dissatisfaction with job duties, wages, or working conditions

Once this information has been brought to light, interviewers must judge to what extent any of the reasons reflect existence of undesirable personality traits and, in turn, what bearing this may have on the individual's ability to satisfy the requirements of the job for which he or she has applied.

If interviewers are not convinced that applicants are telling the truth, they certainly should not challenge them at this point. To do so would be to risk loss of rapport and subsequent lack of spontaneous discussion throughout the remainder of the interview. Rather, they should wait until the interview is nearly concluded—when there is little or nothing to lose. If they are still interested in the candidates' qualifications, they can reintroduce the subject by asking them more directly to elaborate upon their reasons for leaving the job in question.

Reasons for changing jobs tell us a great deal about an individual's *judgment*, and since judgment is directly related to maturity, we also learn a great deal about that important characteristic. Persons who voluntarily leave one job before getting another job are certainly guilty of poor judgment. (It is always more difficult to get a job when one is out of work.) Individuals try to rationalize this situation by saying, "I couldn't very well look for another job while I was working 8 hours a day on that one." This is a poor excuse, since workers can always find a way to get time off for anything as important as an interview for a better job. Interviewers should carefully check reasons for leaving jobs against worker specifications. If a given individual has left jobs because they were "too monotonous" or "involved too much detail," such a person would be a poor risk for a new job that contained those same elements.

An applicant who leaves a series of jobs because of chronic

dissatisfaction with job duties or working conditions may be the type of person who lacks perseverance, maturity, and follow-through. Perhaps unable to take the bitter with the sweet, the applicant quits whenever confronted with anything really difficult or unappealing. If such proves to be the case, a clear indication of immaturity is present. When dissatisfaction appears to be chronic from job to job, the individual concerned may be poorly adjusted emotionally, in the sense of being bitter toward life and taking a negative attitude toward things in general.

On the positive side, reasons for change of jobs often provide a clue to important personality assets. Unwillingness to permit oneself to fall into an occupational rut, desire to raise one's standards of living by making more money, ambition, and eagerness to obtain a broader background experience in a chosen field are a few of the normal motivational factors in moving from one job to another.

While we are on the subject of job changes, it should be pointed out that how individuals *go about getting a job* may be as revealing as why they leave. Some people always seem to depend upon friends or relatives to get them their jobs, but others show great initiative in their efforts to find a better position. Many college kids, for example, complain that they cannot get summer jobs because there is too much competition. The more highly motivated individuals, though, begin their search for a summer job at the time they go home for a Christmas vacation, and by the time summer rolls around they have often landed the kind of job that will do much for their development.

REACTION TO SUPERVISORS AND COWORKERS

If information concerning feelings toward superiors and coworkers does not come out spontaneously, a question such as, "How did you *feel about* your boss?" or "How did you *feel about* the people you worked with there?" usually results in the desired information. Note the wording of these two questions. A question such as, "Did you *like* your boss?" tends to put words in applicants' mouths by pushing them to say that "Yes, I did like my boss." The use of the words "feel about," however, makes any question an open-ended question and is therefore far more useful in obtaining objective information. The responses that applicants give to this question should be carefully checked against the reasons they give for leaving a job.

Where there is an indication of friction, it is important to note the manner in which applicants describe the situation. Do they appear to be frank and reasonably objective in relating these facts? Do they admit that they might have been partially at fault themselves? Or do they take the attitude that their superiors had it in for them, always picked on them for some reason or other, and discriminated against them? This "sour grapes" attitude may be an indication of personality maladjustment. Such people are likely to prove a liability rather than an asset to a company. They are often overly suspicious and overly sensitive and seldom accept responsibility for their own errors.

Then there is the person who boastfully remarks, "The supervisor tried to pull a fast one on me, and I just up and told him to go to hell." This "chip on the shoulder" attitude is sometimes a cover for inner lack of confidence. The braggard is frequently a person lacking in self-confidence who uses this type of behavior, perhaps unconsciously, to hide inadequacies.

It must be remembered, though, that friction may quite possibly be the entire fault of a particular supervisor. Unless there is a recurrence of such incidents of confrontation in other jobs or in other phases of the individual's background, it is dangerous to make any absolute generalization.

Clues as to how well a person gets along with other people often emerge from a discussion of relationships with coworkers. The question, "How did you *feel about* the people there?" is often exceedingly productive. Remarks such as, "I didn't have much in common with them," or "All they seemed to be interested in was sex and drinking," reveal that the applicant really didn't fit in and was not really accepted by coworkers. If this situation prevailed in more than one job, the interviewer would have a right to begin to question the applicant's ability to get along with others. On the other hand, there are persons who appear always to enjoy the people they work with from job to job. They are usually individuals who have developed some good interpersonal skills along the way—skills such as tact, friendliness, and sensitivity to the needs of others.

ATTENDANCE ON LAST JOB

We have mentioned earlier the need to *quantify* in order to obtain hard data. Hence, we do not accept a statement such as, "My attendance there was good." Rather, we try to get the *number of days per year the candidate was absent from work*. We place considerable emphasis on this subject because absenteeism represents such a serious problem in industry today. This is reflected in the remarks of many plant superintendents who say, "Just find me someone who will show up for work everyday; I'll handle the rest." It is obvious that absenteeism is directly related to low productivity. Hence, the better job we do in collecting people who will "show up for work everyday," the more we can contribute to increased productivity.

Since some applicants may lie about their attendance record, interviewers should be alert to such telltale signs as hesitation before the response, squirming in the chair, or other signs of uneasiness. If this is accompanied by attempts to explain away a series of absences by making excuses, interviewers would have to disregard much of an applicant's statements about attendance.

CAREER GOALS

The questions relative to job satisfaction listed on the interview guide usually do an excellent job of getting people to talk about their desires and aspirations. When an applicant runs down and cannot think of anything more to say, the interviewer can stimulate further discussion by utilizing some of the items listed in parentheses after the first career goal question in the guide. The interviewer can say, "What else is important to you? If you had a choice, would you select a job with a fair amount of pressure or one that didn't have so much?" The person who candidly admits to not wanting much pressure on the job may be one who will be satisfied with more routine tasks. This can be probed in another way by saying, "If you had a choice, would you like a job with a considerable amount of responsibility and decision making or one that didn't have so much of this?"

An applicant's response to such a depth question concerning job satisfaction may provide clues to analytical ability and intellectual depth. One person may say, "Oh, I just want a job where I can be happy and make an honest living." Another person may reflect a great deal more discernment and intellectual depth by such a remark as, "I have given this subject a great deal of thought; I am looking primarily for an opportunity to grow and develop—to find the type of job that will provide the greatest challenge and do the most to bring out the best that is in me. Money is, of course, important, but I consider that secondary. Security probably ranks at the bottom of my list since I feel that I can always make a living somewhere." A response such as this tells the interviewer a good bit about the individual's drives and aspirations, as well as about the quality of his or her thinking. The lack of emphasis on security, moreover, may provide a clue to self-confidence.

Discussion of job satisfaction factors presents the interviewer with an excellent opportunity to obtain further confirmation of clues that have come up earlier in the work discussion. For example, having noted some dislike for detail, the interviewer can ask the question, "If you had a choice, would you pick a job with a fair amount of detail or one that did not have so much?" If the applicant seizes upon this with the statement, "Well, for one thing, I certainly do not want to be involved with much detail; I prefer to delegate this to others," the interviewer is presented with additional confirmation of the original hypothesis. If there is reason to suspect that the candidate may be lazy, the interviewer can include in a laundry list question the statement, "Some people want regular hours while others do not mind spending extra time on a job—time that may interfere with family life." The applicant might reply, "I believe that 7 or 8 hours a day on a job is enough for anybody. My family certainly comes first, and I don't intend to let my job interfere." Such a statement may indicate that an individual is unwilling to make present sacrifices for future gains, and this may also provide an additional clue to lack of motivation.

The question of job satisfaction represents such a fruitful area for discussion that at least 4 or 5 minutes should be devoted to this subject. The interviewer then should mentally compare the applicant's expressed desires with the worker specifications of the position in question. Obviously, many young people just out of school may not be able to come up with very much in the way of job satisfaction factors. This should not be held against them since they have not been exposed to enough job situations to enable them to form any real conclusions as to the factors that give them great satisfaction.

The questions, "Why do you want to work for this company?" and "What do you know about us?" may reveal how seriously interested in a job with the company an applicant may be. If he or she has taken the time to investigate such factors as what the company produces, who its major competitors are, or perhaps even something about its financial condition, this would provide a definite indication of maturity as well as seriousness of purpose. It is also a good idea to ask about salary expectations with the thought of trying to find out the extent to which they are realistic. If salary expectations are unrealistically high, there is no way a company is going to be able to keep a candidate happy. When salary expectations are too low, some signs of insecurity or lack of confidence are evident.

The question, "Where do you see yourself 5 years from now?" deals directly with aspiration. If an individual's aspirations are way out of line in terms of abilities, it is a very definite sign of immaturity. If, for example, a woman indicates that she expects to be a manager within a period of 5 years—this in spite of the fact that she is a very shy, introverted, and insecure individual—her aspirations would appear to be unrealistic and hence reflect immaturity. At the same time, most companies like to hire people who have the potential to take on increased responsibility and to move up within the organization. Hence, aspirations within reason represent a favorable factor.

The work history discussion should be concluded with a question concerning the kind of job for which the candidate is looking. In the case of people with some years of specific experience in a given area, this question may be unnecessary since they may be applying for a definite type of work. On the other hand, some younger people may have no specific job in mind. They may say, "I'll be willing to tackle anything you think I might be able to handle." Such responses indicate that the individual has not done sufficient preparation for the job interview. At the very least, such applicants should have made an attempt to find out what kind of jobs might be available and should discuss their qualifications in terms of one or two of these jobs. Failure to have done this kind of preparation represents further clues to immaturity.

As the work history discussion draws to a close, interviewers mentally reflect upon the candidate's total job accomplishment. Has the individual made normal progress in terms of salary? Does the person have a solid background of experience in some specialty? Has the individual shown an ability to assume gradually increased responsibility? If the answer to any of these important questions is negative, the interviewer may begin to have a real reservation concerning the candidate's overall qualifications. In some cases, in fact, the situation may be so clear-cut that the interviewer can decide then and there not to hire the applicant. In such a situation, after a very brief coverage of the candidate's educational background, this interview would be terminated.

EEO AREAS OF CONCERN

1. Many members of minority groups need no special consideration with regard to the interpretation of work history. Their achievement speaks for itself.

2. There are other minority men and women whose work history does not appear very impressive because they have not yet been given an opportunity to demonstrate what they really can do. Since interviewers must try to *screen in* as many minorities as possible, it becomes their job to identify those individuals who have *potential* for greater achievement than their work history would seem to indicate. Some of the following areas may give evidence of such potential:

   a. Probe especially for how each job was obtained, as a possible indication of initiative.

   b. Look for any increased responsibility within a job, even though the job may have been rather routine. For example, the individual may have been promoted to lower levels of supervision such as crew leader, straw boss, or chief clerk.

   c. Give special attention to indications of hard work, such as extremely long hours or physically demanding job duties. A good question here: "To what extent was that job demanding physically?"

   d. Be quick to note significant progress from job to job in terms of more responsibility or higher pay, even though many of the jobs have been routine.

3. Do not be critical of job changes when the new jobs represent

increasingly better situations. We cannot expect a person to stay with a low-level, uninteresting job for any great length of time if advancement is possible elsewhere. In probing for reasons for changing jobs, then, try to determine whether or not the new job really did represent a measurable improvement over the previous one or whether the hopping from job to job is because the person finds it difficult to stay put.

4. In discussing *factors of job satisfaction,* give favorable consideration to the man or woman who seems to have a genuine desire to make something better of himself or herself, even though the individual may not yet have been given much of an opportunity. Persons who have not given up hope deserve more consideration than those who have become cynical or pessimistic.

5. With all applicants, the discussion of *strengths* and *shortcomings* at the end of the interview will be difficult. Interviewers must therefore exercise great patience in developing this information. They will have to do more "pump priming" in terms of introducing strengths and shortcomings that they have observed during the interview. But, once applicants have acquired a definite understanding of what they are expected to do, they can often come up with very valuable information about themselves.

6. In thinking back over the entire work experience, try to determine whether the person was consistently overqualified for many of the jobs held, in the sense that the person could have handled more responsibility if given an opportunity. This situation would seem to indicate that, with special training, the applicant could take over the job under consideration even though his or her work experience may not have been relevant to the job in question.

CHAPTER THIRTEEN

Interpreting Education and Training, Outside Interests, and Self-Evaluation

EDUCATION

In this chapter we address ourselves first to education and training which, of course, includes formal schooling as well as any other learning experiences such as on-the-job training, night school, or correspondence courses. As in the case of work history, education and training occupies many years of an individual's life. Accordingly, it not only indicates fitness for a particular job, but provides clues to attitudes, interests, and goals, many of which can aid in the appraisal of abilities and personality traits. Any discussion of formal school experience is obviously much more meaningful in talking with younger people not long out of school than with older people. Even in the case of the latter, though, a discussion of education is important since the traits that an individual develops while in school often remain throughout life. Moreover, the discussion of educational history frequently provides additional confirming evidence of traits that have been tentatively identified during the discussion of work experience. Thus, the applicant who tends to be lazy on the job can be better understood if the discussion of education and training reveals a similar lack of application in school. In other words, that individual has never been conditioned to hard work and, hence, has never developed strong motivation.

In this chapter, we shall discuss education and training in the order listed on the interview guide. Each item will be discussed not only in terms of its contribution to the individual's educational attainment but also in terms of possible reflection of clues to ability, personality, and motivation.

Structuring the Discussion of Education

With the discussion of work history out of the way, interviewers use a *comprehensive introductory question* to launch the subject of education. The recommended question here is as follows: *"Now tell me about your education and training. I would be interested in the subjects you liked best, those you liked less well, your grades, and your extracurricular activities. Tell me first about high school. What subjects did you like best in high school?"*

Try to observe the order indicated on the interview guide, starting with a discussion of subject preferences, then grades, then extracurricular activities, and finally effort expended. If the candidate jumps ahead to some other aspect of education, *control* the discussion by interrupting the individual with an appropriately timed positive comment and returning the conversation to the appropriate item on the guide. Some people start with extracurricular activities because they are less comfortable in the discussion of their academic pursuits. Even so, they should be encouraged to observe the sequence indicated on the interview guide.

Best- and Least-Liked Subjects

Frequently one of the best clues to an individual's school experience is reaction to a question on best- or least-liked subjects. The person may say, "I liked manual training but didn't care for English, math, history, or foreign languages." Such a response may lend further support to a growing conviction based on other interview or test data that this person likes manual work but is not very good at the kind of abstract thinking needed for many academic subjects. By probing more deeply for the *why* of subject preferences, one can obtain even more relevant data. In response to the question, "What was there about math that gave you a little trouble?" the applicant may say, "Oh, I was completely over my head in that subject. Even though I studied hard, I never could quite understand it." If the worker specifications called for "relatively good mathematical skill," the interviewer will have identified an important shortcoming in this case.

There will naturally be some who appear to have had little preference for one subject as differentiated from another, but a common pattern is a liking for math and science and a dislike of languages and history, or this in reverse. This information can be very helpful in any evaluation of an applicant's interests and abilities in accordance with the requirements of the job. In hiring an applicant for a job where verbal skills are important—such as in the case of a stenographer—preference for such verbal subjects as English and history would of course represent a favorable factor.

Since the educational area represents the best section of the interview for developing clues to *mental ability*, additional probing for why an individual liked a given subject is often revealing. In the case of a person who likes math, one might probe deeper with a question such as, "What was there about math that appealed to you?" This question might elicit a response such as, "I like math because it's a wonderful tool for solving problems. Also, the answers are always either right or wrong, with none of the shades of gray that you find in sociology. There is also an elegance about mathematics in the way everything seems to fit together so precisely." Obviously, a response such as this reflects considerable powers of analysis and intellectual depth.

Grades

This topic can be introduced with the question appearing on the interview guide, "What about grades? Were they average, above average, or somewhat below average?" Note that such a question makes it easier for individuals to admit that their grades were below average. Where grades are indicated as above average, an attempt should be made to determine an applicant's actual ranking in the class. Was it the upper half, upper third, upper quarter, or upper tenth? When an applicant gives a specific number such as "fifth in the class," obviously it is important to find out how many there were in the class.

As we shall see later on, high school grades in themselves are not always indicative of ability. They may reflect outstanding natural ability, or they may have come as a result of extremely hard work. In either case, however, high grades represent an achievement.

If test scores are available, the interviewer's interpretation of grades is greatly facilitated. A high score on a mental ability test means, among other things, that the individual has the ability to learn rapidly, absorbing new information quickly. Hence, that individual would be expected to get good grades in school. If a person with a high mental test score made poor grades in school, the interviewer should be alerted to the possibility that the person did not study very hard. Further probing later on when discussing effort may reveal lack of perseverance, procrastination, or disorganized study habits. Moreover, many gifted people find it possible to get along in school without "cracking a book." Such people not only fail to make the best use of their ability but also develop habits of superficiality, never learning to dig down to the bottom of things. When this habit persists through life, the individual is seldom able to realize her or his full potential.

When an applicant whose mental test score is mediocre claims to have obtained high grades in school, the interviewer is faced with at least three interpretive possibilities. First, there is a possibility that the person may not be telling the truth. Secondly, the academic standards of the school may have been relatively low. Or, thirdly, the person may have studied hard enough to obtain high grades despite a somewhat limited mentality. If the last explanation proves to be the case, the individual is almost certainly hardworking, persevering, and highly motivated to succeed.

Extracurricular Activities

The ability to get along well with others is one that comes largely from practice. When this practice occurs during adolescence, the results can be far-reaching. Most boys and girls, of course, have a circle of close friends with whom they spend most of their leisure hours, but these are usually *friends of their own choosing*—friends with whom they have grown up. When high school students join a club or athletic team, they have to learn to get along with classmates who are often almost complete strangers to them. They soon find that they must make little adjustments in manner in order to merit the approval of the group. This kind of *practice* helps to develop good interpersonal skills at an early age.

Some extracurricular activities also foster the development of leadership. A girl elected president of her class, for example, is confronted with responsibilities that are entirely new to her. She is naturally anxious to show up well in the eyes of other members of the class and, therefore, takes particular pains to do the best job she can. In the course of shouldering these responsibilities, she often matures perceptibly, acquiring new poise, learning how to handle the more difficult people, and developing the kind of infectious enthusiasm that sparks an organization.

Participation in sports often results in more than physical development. Such activity fosters the development of competitive spirit, cooperation, and the ability to serve as an effective member of a team.

In the case of persons who did not participate in extracurricular activities, it is often useful to probe for the why. They may indicate that they were too shy, self-conscious, or backward. Such persons may have changed substantially over the years, but the chances are very good that certain vestiges of these shortcomings remain today. Occasionally, we find persons who say that they did not participate in student activities because they did not care very much for the type of classmates with whom they were associated. Further probing may reveal that this was a possible indication of snobbishness, intolerance, or a sour grape attitude.

Effort

The order of the items appearing under education on the interview guide is intentional and very important. Were we to ask about "effort" immediately after discussing grades, for example, we might not get an objective response, particularly if the grades were not very good. For that reason, we wait until we have changed the subject completely by discussing extracurricular activities. Then we slip in the question found on the interview guide, "How conscientious a student were you in high school? Did you study about as hard as the average person, a little harder, or perhaps not quite so hard?"

When a person frankly admits to having studied hard, try to get a more definitive response with such a question as, "How many hours did you usually study during the evening?"

The question as to the amount of effort expended in high school can provide excellent clues to both intellect and motivation. If a candidate attained good grades in a school with high academic standards without working particularly hard, good mental ability can be assumed. On the other hand, if high school grades were not better than the average despite unusually hard study, there would seem to be some question about the level of mental ability. In the latter case the individual, however, can be given credit for strong motivation. It is not unusual for such a person to say, "I really had to work for everything I got. My subjects never came easily to me." The negative aspects of such a comment should be "played down" by the interviewer with a statement such as, "You deserve a great deal of credit for putting first things first."

As noted earlier, grades in themselves are not particularly meaningful unless we know whether they resulted from high natural ability or unusually hard study. For this reason, interviewers should never try to interpret grades without first having discovered the amount of effort required to get those grades.

Students Who Do Not Graduate from High School

Many applicants for factory jobs will have left high school without graduating. In that case, it is important to probe for the reason why. A question such as, "How did you happen to leave school?" will serve to introduce this discussion. Studies have shown that many youths leave school because of insufficient mental capacity to handle the academic work. Rarely will the applicant admit to being "too dumb to pass." But a low intelligence test score, together with any indications of dislike for academic subjects, is a rather sure indication of difficulty. If really good rapport has been established, the individual may even say, "I really could not handle that situation. The teacher always picked on me, and the other kids always laughed at me. I couldn't take it anymore." When such information is brought to light, the interviewer naturally refers to the worker specifications. If the individual is being considered for a routine assembly job, below-average intelligence would probably not be a handicap. However, if the entry-level job required a person with potential for moving up in the organization to jobs of greater responsibility, the finding of below-average mental capacity would represent a serious shortcoming.

Some young people of average or even above-average intelligence leave school to go to work, even though they have no real difficulty in passing subjects and have families who are well able to support them while they complete school. In such cases, poor judgment and immaturity are usually the underlying reasons. Some adolescents are easily swayed by their more dominant peers. When the latter decide to quit school, the former often tag along. Some of these individuals remain overly dependent upon others throughout their lives and, hence, never develop any real potential for leadership. There are some legitimate reasons for leaving school, however, reasons such as pregnancy or early marriage.

Special Training Since Leaving High School

If the candidate has gone on to college after completing high school, the interviewer would, of course, investigate the college experience with respect to subject preferences, grades, extracurricular activities, and the amount of effort expended. Most candidates for entry-level jobs probably would not have had the advantage of college, but many will have had other important educational and training experiences.

Many jobs are open only to those with a specified number of months experience *on the job.* Ordinarily no amount of classroom work will make up for lack of training on the job. Thus, as a qualification for a turret lathe operator, the job specification would probably list at least 3 months on-the-job experience on a turret lathe. The operation of machine tools can only be learned by actually running the given machine. Years of experience on an internal grinder, for instance, cannot be accepted as qualifications for operation of an engine lathe unless there has been some additional job training on the lathe itself. However, the grinder's knowledge of tolerances, metals, and machine feeds would undoubtedly help master the operation of an engine lathe more quickly than someone without this background.

We need to know about any special training since leaving high school not only as a means of obtaining a complete record of education and training but also as a possible reflection of personality makeup. What extension course, night-school, seminar, or correspondence training have the individuals taken that will enable them to better perform the job they desire? Those seeking to improve their job skills by attending class at night after having done their day's work are usually the type that "want to get somewhere" and are willing to make the necessary sacrifice to obtain their goal. Such self-improvement programs represent tangible evidence of ambition, maturity, and capacity for constructive activity. Few people who begin correspondence courses ever finish them. Therefore, the individual who *does* complete a correspondence course over a period of months must be given credit for unusual self-discipline and perseverance.

Though classwork is the more common means of self-improvement, some workers carry out rather comprehensive programs of self-study under the guidance of their immediate supervisor. Thus, the shop clerk, at the suggestion of a supervisor, studies recommended material on time study in the evening at home. Frequently, the information acquired at night can be applied to work the next day. In this manner, the clerk may eventually become capable of making time studies of a few simple operations. This person has conducted a program of self-improvement of as much significance as, or perhaps greater significance than, that of a person who has completed formal classwork in the subject.

However, there are certain people who seem to take courses without any real purpose. Unless the study is tied up to a vocational objective, results are not as significant. Where persons have taken extension training which is related to the requirements of the job they are seeking, this should weigh heavily in their favor. Courses taken under these conditions are likely to have contributed greatly to the individuals' backgrounds because they were taken *with a purpose*. Perhaps more significant still, they reflect a positive interest in the job for which the applicants have been preparing and are now applying.

Mental Review of Educational Experience

Just as interviewers mentally review the work experience when that area is concluded, so they mentally evaluate the applicants' educational experience. As applicants conclude their discussions of their education and training, interviewers ask themselves certain questions. Does an applicant have sufficient formal education in terms of the demands of the worker specifications? Does a candidate have the required math or mechanical training? Did an individual perform in high school about as well as might be expected in light of what that person has to work with? Does the high school experience reflect particularly good mental capacity, strong motivation, leadership, or perhaps unusually good ability to get along with others?

OUTSIDE INTERESTS AND HOBBIES

Most applicants can be encouraged to talk about leisure time activities by some casual remark such as, "What are some of the things you like to do outside of working hours?" This is an important area for discussion because it sometimes supplies clues to such important factors as mental ability, ability to get along with others, energy level, and leadership potential. As noted earlier, this area is of particular importance in evaluating homemakers and recent high school graduates—people without much in the way of industrial experience.

Participation in community affairs should be thoroughly evaluated. In how many such activities does the individual engage? How many hours a week are spent in these pursuits? Has the individual assumed responsibility for leadership in any club or community groups? Individuals who take their community responsibilities seriously usually reflect the attributes of a solid citizen. They are more likely to be responsible, concerned, and willing to get involved, and, as with extracurricular activities in school, community participation provides an opportunity to *practice* skills in getting along with others. People who spend a considerable amount of time (try to get the specific number of hours) on community activities are frequently people with high energy. In addition to working all day on their regular jobs, they still have sufficient energy and stamina left over for community affairs. This tells us a great deal about their drive and motivation.

Many people seem naturally to gravitate to positions of leadership in activities outside their jobs. This means that other people look to them for direction. It may also mean that they have the potential for moving up to a position of leadership in their job situation.

It is also helpful to ask about reading with such a question as, "What about reading? Do you have any time for that, or do other things crowd it out?" If the response is positive, the interviewer should find out what kinds of books the person reads and how many such books that person reads per month. In general, there is some correlation between reading habits and general mental ability. Brighter people definitely do more reading than those not so gifted. Hence, if a person reads some books of a more serious nature, such as good fiction, nonfiction, and biographies, that person probably has a relatively good mind.

Since America is very sports-conscious, many applicants will be found to participate in such sports as golf, tennis, handball, racquetball, and softball. This obviously represents an asset since most sports participants try to keep in good shape physically. A healthy person may have fewer absences from work and may be able to devote more energy to the job. Participation in sports can also provide clues to energy level. People who are able to engage in sports that are physically demanding, after working a full day on their jobs, certainly have a high level of energy.

Some hobbies reflect a penchant for detail. Persons engaged in such activities as model building, crocheting, and dressmaking are normally those who like to see things done with accuracy and precision. They have the kind of temperament which enables them to spend hours at a confining task. This obviously has its implications for placement on a job in industry.

SELF-EVALUATION

At the end of the interview it is helpful to ask applicants to discuss their strengths and shortcomings. This often enables the interviewer to obtain additional confirming evidence of assets and shortcomings that have come to light during the interview. Also, with certain individuals, such a discussion enables them to acquire greater self-insight. Most people have never given any comprehensive, systematic thought to their own strengths and shortcomings. A discussion of this kind then often clarifies their thinking about those traits and abilities they possess in abundance as well as the characteristics that need some improvement for their further development. Questions concerning strengths and shortcomings found on the interview guide should prove most helpful.

Helping Applicants Discuss Their Strengths

The interviewer introduces the subject of strengths with the laundry list question, "If we were to contact your previous employers, what do you think they would say about your strengths? Would they say that you worked harder than the average person, got along better with people, had a better attendance record, were more reliable—what would they say?" Immediately after the applicant has mentioned each asset, the interviewer should *lubricate the situation* by giving the candidate a verbal pat on the back. If the individual mentions being a hard worker, for example, and if abundant evidence of this trait has already been seen, the interviewer might say, "I am sure you are a very hard worker, and that is a wonderful asset to have." On the other hand, if some doubt exists about the individual's motivation, the interviewer would simply nod and ask the applicant to indicate some other strengths, resolving to reintroduce the subject of hard work later on when talking about the individual's shortcomings.

Since most people find it somewhat difficult to list their real assets, interviewers should stimulate the discussion by pointing out one or two strengths already observed during the interview. They might say, "Well, I have observed that you seem to get along unusually well with people, and this of course is a tremendous asset in any job." After priming the pump with one or two such observations, interviewers should pass the conversational ball back to the candidates, asking them to discuss some of their other strong points. If the candidates seem unable to come up with any additional assets on their own, make use of the *calculated pause*, in this way giving them an opportunity to organize their thoughts. If, after 6 or 8 seconds, they are still unable to come up with anything, interviewers should "take them off the hook" by introducing another asset observed during the interview. In some cases, a considerable amount of pump priming may be necessary before candidates begin to talk about their strengths, but interviewers should wait them out, using as much patience as they can muster.

Interviewers should stay with the subject of strengths until they have drawn out a list of at least 8 to 10 assets and have spent at least 5 minutes in so doing. Otherwise, applicants may be quite reluctant subsequently to discuss their shortcomings. Remember, people usually feel confident about discussing their shortcomings only if they feel that the interviewer has a full appreciation of all their major strengths.

There are some applicants, of course, whose recitation of their own assets has to be taken with a grain of salt, particularly if they have shown any previous tendency to overplay their hand or to withhold important information. Remember, too, that candidates are trying to get a job and are therefore anxious to sell themselves.

Helping Applicants Discuss Their Shortcomings

Interviewers introduce this subject with a question on the interview guide: "What would your previous employers say that you could improve? No one is perfect; we all have some things we could improve. Would they say you could use more patience, do a better job of getting to work on time, control your temper a little better, be a little more aggressive—what would they say?"

In discussing development needs, always use the word "shortcomings" rather than "weaknesses" or "liabilities." The last two words carry the connotation that the trait may be so serious that the individual can do very little about it. The word "shortcomings," on the other hand, implies that the trait is just a little short of what it might desirably be and, hence, the person may be able to improve it or eliminate it. Always talk, too, in terms of "ways in which you can improve yourself." Thus, instead of saying, "What are some other shortcomings?" it is better to say, "What are some of the other ways in which you might improve yourself?" Experience has shown that people are much more willing to discuss traits that they can *improve* than characteristics in which they are deficient.

Immediately after each shortcoming has been mentioned, the interviewer should play it down, as has been done with any other unfavorable information throughout the interview. When an individual admits, for example, the need to develop more self-confidence, the interviewer might say, "Well, confidence is a trait that many people need to develop further. I am sure that you can develop more of this as you acquire more experience." When a person admits a rather serious shortcoming, such as a quick temper, the interviewer can play this down by complimenting the person for having recognized it and for having faced up to it. A comment such as the following would be appropriate: "You deserve a lot of credit for being able to recognize this. And because you have recognized it, you probably have already taken certain steps toward eliminating it."

The interviewer primes the pump in this area by means of the *double-edged question.* Thus, having noted some lack of initiative, the interviewer might say, "What about initiative? Do you think you have as much of this as you would like to have, or is this something that you can improve a little bit?" Such a question makes it easy for a person to admit shortcomings, and if a question still exists about the candidate's work habits, the interviewer may say, "What about work habits? Do you think that you usually work as hard as you should, or is this something that you could improve a little bit?"

For the most part, indicated shortcomings can be taken pretty much at face value. Seldom will one draw attention to shortcomings that do not really exist.

The interviewer's role in the self-evaluation discussion is a critical one. Trying to stimulate the discussion by introducing assets or shortcomings that are not part of the applicant's makeup risks a loss of the applicant's respect. On the other hand, introducing traits that go to the very heart of the individual's personality and motivational patterns usually heightens respect for the interviewer.

The Value of the Self-Evaluation Technique

As noted above, this technique can be of considerable value to both the applicant and the interviewer. The applicant gains by getting a clearer picture of personal strengths and development needs, thus acquiring greater insight; the interviewer gains by frequently being able to get more documentary evidence concerning the candidate's overall qualifications.

When interviewers are able to get applicants to agree with them on the presence or absence of certain traits, this obviously provides strong support for the original diagnosis. For example, an interviewer who has seen several clues to insecurity throughout the interview waits expectantly for some indication of this in the candidate's self-evaluation. If lack of self-confidence is spontaneously admitted or admitted as a result of probing with a double-edged question, the interviewer has, of course, developed further confirmation of the original hypothesis.

There are occasions, too, when applicants will mention a trait that may not have consciously crystallized in the interviewer's mind but which seems abundantly in evidence as soon as it is verbalized. In other words, the interviewer may have been only vaguely aware of the trait, but when the applicant mentions it specifically, a number of clues immediately come to mind that actually pointed in that direction earlier in the interview. If the applicant had not mentioned this trait, the interviewer might not have included it in the overall decision.

When a candidate mentions an asset or shortcoming for which the interviewer has seen no clues, it is advisable to ask the individual to elaborate. Subsequent remarks may convince the interviewer that the applicant actually possesses the trait in question, thus bringing to light valuable information that otherwise might have been missed.

EEO AREAS OF CONCERN

1. Make sure that educational standards (high school graduation, for example) established for selection of new employees are consistent with the educational attainment of employees already working on those jobs in the plant or office. An artificially established educational standard may screen out a disproportionate number of minorities, and this is unfair (and cannot be defended) if some of the workers already on the job do not meet the new standard. (New educational requirements can only be established if the technology changes.)

2. Hard and fast grade requirements, such as a B average, are difficult to defend. Many factors affect grades, such as an outside job, an inordinate number of extracurricular activities, or the academic standards of schools attended. Do not be overly critical of low grades before giving an applicant a chance to explain.

3. Even if educational requirements can be defended, an organization must consider the extent to which additional recruitment may be necessary to provide a sufficient number of qualified minorities and women to meet its EEO commitments.

4. The effect of educational requirements on the handicapped must also be considered. Many handicapped persons have not been able to obtain a formal education because of their inability to attend classes due to architectural barriers. In such cases, try to determine if the individual has obtained an informal education that is in any way comparable through self-study or other means.

CHAPTER FOURTEEN

The Three M's

In our chapters on interpretation we have discussed a wide variety of personality and ability factors—so many, in fact, that it now seems logical to pull them together in some order of relative importance. Experience over the years has shown that three factors take on by far the most importance. We shall refer to these as the three M's—motivation, maturity, and mental ability. These three factors prove so important because they include so many of the characteristics we look for in a steady, productive employee. Applicants who are well-motivated, mature emotionally, and reasonably intelligent represent good candidates for some kind of job in any given organization. The specific job for which they are qualified, of course, depends upon such secondary factors as relevance of work experience, education and training, adaptability, and ability to get along with others.

In this chapter, we shall call attention to the reasons why motivation, maturity, and mental ability occupy a place of such importance in our evaluation of any candidate. And, at the risk of repetition, we shall review the major clues which help to identify these three factors, bringing together materials from a number of the previous chapters.

MOTIVATION

In terms of selecting hourly workers for the plant and office, motivation probably represents the single most important factor to be considered. So many office managers and plant superintendents tell us that many of their people take little interest in their work, have poor work standards, and look for every opportunity to escape from their work by frequent visits to the restrooms, extended lunch breaks, or failure to show up for work altogether. Of course, we take the view that, once the company casts away indiscriminate hiring in favor of a well-designed selection program, it will find that it *is* possible to select highly motivated workers. This can be done by placing special emphasis on the factors that follow.

Conditioning to Work

People who have become accustomed to working hard establish this as a habit pattern, a pattern of behavior that often extends throughout their entire lives. We look for clues to this important trait by probing for likes and dislikes on various jobs—including summer jobs while attending school—number of hours worked, the extent to which any previous jobs have included hard manual labor, and the kinds of things that give the individual job satisfaction.

As surprising as it may seem to some, there are still people around who enjoy working, who work hard as a matter of course, and who are anxious to make something of themselves.

High Energy Level

As in the case of most other attributes, energy represents a force that some people have in abundance and others have to a much lesser extent. No one knows for sure why this is so, but quite probably both heredity and environment are responsible. At any rate, energy represents the spark or driving force that makes the human machine go. Thus, people with a great deal of energy find it quite possible to carry out a demanding job during the day and still have energy left for equally demanding outside activities during the evening.

It has been the authors' observation that most individuals who make their way to the top are people of inordinate energy. In fact, many of them are "workaholics"—people who spend some 10 to 12 hours a day on the job and even take some work home with them at night. Of course, we do not expect to find many workaholics applying for hourly jobs, but we nevertheless find applicants whose energy level is appreciably above that of the average individual. These are the people who make interviewers stand up and take notice.

With proper training, interviewers pick up clues to energy in all areas of the interview. In the work history, for example, they give special attention to whether applicants are able to handle enervating jobs without undue difficulty or to whether such jobs seem to have drained them of their energy and stamina. A job such as mason's helper, which involves pushing heavy wheelbarrows full of cement much of the day, is one that quickly filters out low-stamina workers. Only individuals with appreciable energy and stamina are able to carry out such a job over a period of some time.

The educational history represents another area where clues to energy may be found. High school students who carry a full academic load and still have sufficient energy for extracurricular activities and perhaps a part-time job are quite obviously individuals with considerable energy and stamina. If they do this for only a few months, it may not be altogether significant, but if they carry on these myriad activities over a much longer period of time, they certainly qualify as high-energy people.

In discussing outside interests and hobbies, interviewers are equally on the lookout for evidence of energy. They are obviously impressed by people who have the energy to participate in physically demanding sports, such as handball, racquetball, and tennis, after putting in a hard day's work on the job. The discussion of outside interests and hobbies sometimes reveals a second job. There are people who, in addition to their factory jobs, "do a little farming on the side." Anyone who has ever made hay, weeded vegetables, or "mucked out" horse stalls knows how physically demanding "a little farming" can be. Interestingly enough, some people seem to have the energy to carry out all sorts of activities in addition to their job, while others complain about being completely "bushed" at the end of a normal workday.

Initiative

The self-starter is highly prized by the plant and office alike. Employees who exercise initiative obviously require less supervision. They have the necessary drive to begin things on their own, without having to be told. As a result, they accomplish more in a given day and contribute appreciably to productivity.

Interviewers get many clues to initiative by asking applicants how they got each of their jobs. As we mentioned earlier, some people always seem to rely upon friends and relatives to get them better jobs. People with initiative dig out their own sources. They send out résumés to carefully selected companies, follow this up with telephone calls, and manage to set up a considerable number of interviews. Many blue-collar workers go from plant to plant, asking for work and filing applications. Some young people in high school, moreover, exercise a great deal of initiative in getting the kind of summer job that will do most for their development and pay them the best money.

Conscientiousness

Highly motivated people are usually conscientious as well. This means that they have high work standards, in the sense that they derive personal satisfaction from seeing a job well-done. It stands to reason, too, that conscientious employees have better attendance records. Instead of taking the day off at the slightest indication of physical disability, they show up for work because they know that their supervisors count on them to help get the job done.

Again, clues to conscientiousness often pop out as a result of the discussion of likes and dislikes. A man might say that he enjoyed working for his boss because the latter had high standards and insisted that "everything be done just so," or he might indicate that he liked a given job because he was given sufficient time "to do it right." A woman might be critical of some of her coworkers because they were inclined to "do a sloppy job." By implication, that remark would indicate that her own standards are appreciably higher.

Indications of conscientiousness may also be reflected in responses to the question on factors of job satisfaction. Candidates may indicate that they enjoy working with detail and appreciate a job that requires accuracy and thoroughness. Reactions to the educational experience often provide further clues to conscientiousness. Some individuals make every effort to get their assignments done on time, while others wait until the last minute.

MATURITY

As important as motivation is, it cannot do the job alone. Successful, productive workers are also *mature*. People may work to the point of becoming workaholics, but unless they exercise good *judgment* and have some idea of who they are and where they are going, they will almost invariably fall by the wayside.

Judgment

People who lack judgment often make the wrong choice when confronted with important alternatives at critical stages of their lives. They may take the wrong kind of job, may leave jobs for the wrong reasons, or may do a poor job of planning their personal and financial affairs. Immature employees are often accident-prone. They take chances with equipment and with their own personal safety—chances that mature people, with better judgment, would never take.

As implied above, clues to judgment are often brought to light as a result of probing for the reasons why candidates took various jobs as well as the reasons why they left them. Men and women who accept jobs without knowing anything more about them than what they pay are obviously immature people. People who take evening courses "without rhyme or reason," just because a neighbor may be taking such courses, may be demonstrating poor planning or judgment in their use of leisure time. Finally, people who overextend themselves, attempting to engage in too many outside activities, also show a lack of judgment.

Willingness to Make Present Sacrifices for Future Gains

Mature individuals have the kind of self-discipline that enables them to make themselves do things which have to be done but which may not be particularly pleasant. We have mentioned earlier that, given their personal preferences, few people would probably choose to work on shifts or spend their workday in an environment involving heat, noise, and other hazards. They usually agree to work under these conditions because they will earn more money and, hence, will be able to buy a better home later on or to put their children through college. In so doing, they show a willingness to make present sacrifices for future gains. Most people go into such jobs "with their eyes open," knowing full well what they are going to have to adjust to and accepting the situation because of the monetary reward.

In their attempts to assess this aspect of maturity, interviewers scrutinize work history, education, and outside interests for any indications of "willingness to put first things first." When they find an individual who has done shift work or worked in a noisy, dirty, hazardous environment, they probe to see how well that person adjusted to this type of situation. The person who says, "I hated every minute of it," is probably one who should not be selected for a similar environment again. But the individual who says, "I can't say I really liked it, but I learned to live with it and found that it was well worth any sacrifice involved. I have a brand-new home to show for it," is one who has "been there before" and should be able to adapt to a similar situation again.

Willingness to "Stay Put"

Mature individuals are people who have sufficiently broad horizons to look at all aspects of a given situation before making a move. They are not likely to be job-hoppers therefore, because they do not make decisions on the spur of the moment. For instance, instead of quitting a job because it tends to be monotonous or because they really do not like their supervisor, they decide to stay on because the chances for advancement to a more-demanding job with a different supervisor appear to be relatively good. Job-hoppers, on the other hand, often have "short fuses," become easily discouraged, or always think that the next job will be the "right" one for them. They seldom look at themselves critically, always believing that the other person is at fault.

Self-Insight

When responses to questions on strengths, shortcomings, and factors of job satisfaction reveal a person with self-insight, that person is mature. The ability to accept oneself and to be aware of one's limitations is an indication of both maturity and emotional adjustment. The person, for example, who is extremely shy and introverted and recognizes that these traits preclude promotion to supervision is one who has self-perception. Instead of becoming bitter about lack of promotion to supervision, that person may strive to excel as an individual contributor and become much happier as a result. Reasonable vocational goals, then, represent further indications of maturity.

Relationships with People

The mature person is also one who exercises self-control, and this, of course, enhances that individual's relationships with people. It is the immature individuals who take pride in telling people off or insisting upon doing everything their own way. Mature people, on the other hand, are able to control their tempers and wait for a more opportune time to discuss differences.

Interviewers usually find it relatively easy to spot individuals who lack "people skills." Such individuals report chronic dissatisfaction with peers and supervisors alike, and they often find it difficult to fit in when introduced to situations involving new people and a strange environment.

MENTAL ABILITY

Some people who are highly motivated and mature as well never make much job progress because they do not have sufficient mental ability. We have mentioned earlier that lack of reasonably good mental capacity may not be a particularly serious shortcoming in applicants for hourly jobs, particularly if such jobs have a high degree of monotony. It is generally accepted that brighter people have more difficulty adjusting to monotonous jobs than do less-gifted individuals.

The introduction of higher technology and automation in the plant and office probably means that many of the routine jobs will be eliminated, however. This means that even beginning jobs will require more skill and perhaps a higher degree of abstract thinking. Most companies today, moreover, look for workers who are promotable. They want individuals who have the capacity to move up to more demanding positions. The key ingredient to promotability, more highly skilled jobs, and jobs requiring some abstract thinking is mental ability. People tend to stay on the lower rungs of the ladder if they are not able to learn quickly, to plan their work effectively, or to be attentive to the operation of complex machinery. Candidates for jobs in the modern office setup today are expected not only to be able to type and file but to show potential for computer programming and the operation of word processors.

We have pointed out earlier that an aptitude testing service is available at the state employment office for jobs for which the U.S. Employment Service has validated specific tests. Where tests are not available, interviewers must do the best they can to evaluate an applicant's mental ability and math, verbal, or mechanical aptitude. With practice, they can learn to do quite a good job of evaluating these abilities.

Grades in Relation to Effort

Although grades per se are not a reliable indication of mental ability, they become significantly more reliable when considered in light of the amount of effort the individual expended in order to get those grades, particularly if the academic standards of the school attended are taken into consideration. Thus, a person who attains relatively high grades in a school of acknowledged high academic standards without having to expend great effort can be assumed to be a reasonably bright individual. In sharp contrast, a person who is unable to obtain better-than-average grades in a school of questionable academic standards, despite a great amount of effort and long hours of study, is quite probably somewhat limited intellectually.

Subject Likes and Dislikes

Some individuals show a liking for shop courses (a mechanical aptitude) but have more difficulty with the more abstract academic subjects such as mathematics, physics, chemistry, and English literature. Such individuals may be quite qualified for certain routine plant jobs but are probably not very gifted intellectually. Likewise, since people quite naturally tend to do best on subjects that they like, it may be assumed that individuals showing a preference for English, history, and foreign languages probably have a relatively good verbal aptitude and persons showing a preference for math and science probably have a reasonably good math aptitude.

Reasons for Leaving High School

Studies have shown that many boys and girls leave high school without graduating because they can't handle the academic work. This is, of course, not true in every case since some people leave to get jobs in order to support themselves or help their families, some leave because of disciplinary problems, and some are not encouraged by their families to stay in school. Nevertheless, in the case of applicants who have not finished high school, interviewers should be alert to the possibility of below-average mental capacity. This is particularly true in individuals who dislike academic subjects or have relatively low grades. When interviewers have succeeded in building good rapport, the true reason for leaving high school will undoubtedly surface.

Quality of Response to In-Depth Questions

Although interviewers should be alert to the quality of applicants' responses throughout the discussion, they should give particular attention to certain items on the interview guide. These items are factors of job satisfaction and the self-evaluation section (strengths and shortcomings) at the end of the interview. These areas—perhaps more than any of the others—require a great amount of concentration, analysis, and in-depth thinking on the part of the applicant. Thus, applicants whose responses in these areas reveal analytical power, perception, self-insight, and intellectual depth are quite obviously individuals with above-average intelligence.

When persons seem unable to respond appropriately in the areas noted above, however, they should not be immediately written off as unintelligent. Most individuals have never been called upon to evaluate themselves and, hence, find these areas difficult. There are cases, too, where individuals do possess analytical ability but cannot communicate well enough to reveal this ability. In such cases, interviewers have to rely upon other clues. For example, if a person has done outstandingly well in such subjects as higher mathematics, physics, or chemistry, a reasonable degree of analytical ability can be assumed or the person would not have been able to master these subjects.

It will be seen from the above discussion that a reasonable degree of motivation, maturity, and mental ability is an absolute essential for success in most jobs. In fact, those individuals who are seriously lacking in any one of the three M's quite probably represent a poor risk for employment. As soon as an interviewer becomes absolutely certain that a given applicant is seriously lacking in any one of the three M's, he or she should find a way to terminate the interview as gracefully as possible.

CHAPTER FIFTEEN

Making the Employment Decision and Writing the Interview Report

PERSONALITY AND ABILITY CONFORMATIONS

We have noted throughout the chapters on interpretation that interviewers—with proper training and practice—will normally know whether or not they wish to hire an applicant by the time that individual leaves the room. This is because they have been picking up clues to behavior throughout the discussion of work history, education, and outside interests and, by the end of the interview, have acquired sufficient hard, factual documentation to support an objective employment decision. Even so, reference to the personality and ability conformations found on page 208 should enable an interviewer to become more *definite* with respect to the employment decision. Also, the write-up of the case will help the interviewer to decide whether an applicant is "best-qualified," "qualified," or "not qualified."

It is suggested that interviewers copy the personality and ability conformations on page 208 onto an 8½- by 11-inch card for easy reference at the end of all their interviews. This would permit

PERSONALITY AND ABILITY CONFORMATIONS

Primary

Motivation
- Energy
- Willingness to work
- Initiative
- Conscientiousness
- Self-discipline
- Perseverance
- Aspirations

Maturity
- Judgment
- Reasonableness of vocational goals
- Knowledge of self
- Disinclination to rationalize
- Awareness of limitations
- Ability to "take the bitter with the sweet"

Mental Ability
- Verbal aptitude
- Math aptitude
- Ability to learn quickly
- Ability to plan
- Attentiveness

Secondary

Relevance of Prior Jobs
- Similar duties
- Similar working conditions
- Shift work
- Usual required hand or machine tools

Educational Relevance
- Sufficient formal schooling
- Required on-the-job training
- Sufficient math courses
- Required skills training (typing, shorthand, etc.)

People Skills
- Tact
- Empathy
- Sensitivity to the needs of others
- Friendliness
- Cooperativeness

Leadership
- Assertiveness
- Self-confidence
- Tough-mindedness
- Ability to communicate
- Enthusiasm
- Well-organized approach

Character
- Honesty
- Reliability
- Personal value system

Adaptability

Technical Ability
- Mechanical aptitude
- Math aptitude
- Attention to detail
- Ability to read blueprints

them to decide the extent to which an applicant, first of all, possesses the three M's—listed as "primary qualifications." They should then check out the applicant on the "secondary qualifications," relevance of work experience, required education and training, people skills, leadership potential, character, adaptability, and technical ability.

Tough-Mindedness

In the previous chapter, we discussed all aspects of the three M's, item by item, and throughout our chapters on interpretation we have discussed most of the factors listed under secondary qualifications. There is one trait listed under leadership potential, though, to which we have not given much attention—tough-mindedness. This is normally defined as a willingness to stand up and be counted, a willingness to effect confrontations with people when necessary, and a willingness to make difficult decisions involving people for the good of the organization. Clues to this trait will be found in the extent to which individuals have stood up to peers or perhaps even to supervisors when differences of opinion have occurred. Tough-mindedness is also reflected in an individual's willingness to state an opinion, even though knowing the opinion is unpopular. If individuals have already had some supervisory experience, it is helpful to ask how they *feel about* disciplinary problems. Many supervisors are too soft, in the sense that they take the easy way out. Thus, they fail to discharge an individual even when the person is obviously either unqualified or a troublemaker.

Adaptability

Although we have mentioned this trait from time to time throughout the book, we call attention to it once again because *it is so important in hiring people without previous experience.* Thus, adaptability is of particular importance in evaluating homemakers who are entering the job market for the first time or applicants recently graduated from high school. Interviewers should carefully scrutinize such factors as summer jobs while attending school, the entire educational experience, and outside activities for clues to adaptability. Look particularly for how much time it takes the individual to adapt to situations which are entirely new. Interviewers should also be concerned about people without experience who show clear signs of inflexibility. One cannot be inflexible and adaptable at the same time.

WRITING THE INTERVIEW REPORT

We have noted in earlier chapters that interviewers must file a report on every single individual interviewed, whether hired or rejected. EEO regulations require such a report, and personnel departments are therefore obligated to maintain a record of the reasons for either hiring or rejecting every applicant. But, as pointed out earlier, this is only good personnel practice anyway. Individuals who have been rejected might appear at the employment office sometime in the future, and if no records are available, they may have to be put through the entire employment process again.

We would like to emphasize again the importance of equipping interviewers with dictating equipment. Once they have learned to utilize this equipment, they find it possible to dictate an interview report in a very few minutes, immediately after the applicant leaves the room. In that way, report-writing chores do not accumulate—to the point where interviewers cannot remember specific applicants well enough to keep all such reports from sounding almost the same.

However, there is another more important reason for writing interview reports. Actually, the write-up of the case represents an integral part of the interviewing process. Experience has shown that, as interviewers record their results, their thinking crystallizes with respect to the applicants' qualifications. The write-up of the case, therefore, represents an extension of decision making. As interviewers record their findings, they become more and more definite in their value judgments and, hence, are normally able to assign a more precise rating to the candidates' qualifications. The case write-up forces interviewers to weigh all the relevant factors, and, as a consequence, they are usually in a much better position to decide whether applicants' qualifications merit an average rating, a well-above-average rating, or perhaps an excellent rating.

Interview Report Form

To facilitate report writing, we have provided two sample interview report forms (see pages 211 to 213). The report form requires that interviewers list applicants' assets and shortcomings. Once that has been done, they draw upon the list of assets and shortcomings to write the summary paragraph.

The preparation of the interview report, then, represents a logical next step to the study of the personality and ability conformation data. Once the interviewers have satisfied themselves as to the extent to which an applicant satisfies the primary and secondary qualifications, they are in a position to list an applicant's major strengths and shortcomings. And, having done this, it is a relatively easy next step to discuss strengths and shortcomings in the summary paragraph.

The Summary Paragraph

In the summary paragraph the interviewers include major strengths in the first paragraph and the most serious shortcomings in the second paragraph. In the third paragraph they show how they *resolve* this situation by indicating whether the assets outweigh the shortcomings or vice versa. This resolution dictates the overall rating. If the interviewer decides that the assets and shortcomings are about equally weighted, an "average" overall rating would be indicated. If the interviewer decides that the assets clearly outweigh the shortcomings, an "above average" rating would be justified, and if the interviewer decides that the assets *substantially* outweigh the shortcomings, an "excellent" rating would be appropriate. Ratings of "excellent" or "above average" mean that an applicant is "best-qualified." A rating of "average" designates a "qualified" candidate, and ratings of "below average" or "poor" signify that the applicant is "not qualified."

In making these evaluations and overall ratings, the interviewer must keep the applicable worker specifications clearly in mind. Applicants may measure up overall as good employment risks in the sense that they have an abundance of the three M's. However, if they do not have some of the *specific* requirements of the worker specifications for a particular job, such as specific related experience, specific training, or liking for fine detail, they would still have to be rejected for that particular job. With the knowledge that an applicant represents a basically good potential employee, however, an interviewer would make every effort to try to find another job for which the individual was better-suited.

INTERVIEW RATING FORM

Name   James F. Waters   Date   9/14/82

Interviewed for   Machinist   Interviewer   F. T. Brazzy

Summary of Assets	Summary of Liabilities
Above-average intelligence	Not much leadership potential
- learns quickly	- not forceful
- quite analytical	- lacks self-confidence
- able to plan and organize	- not tough-minded
	- does not communicate very well; not very verbal
Good technical ability	- somewhat introverted; something of a loner
- excellent mechanical aptitude	
- good math aptitude	

(continued)

- critical in his thinking
- good attention to detail

Very good motivation
  - works hard
  - conscientious
  - high work standards

Mature for age
  - knows what he wants
  - good self-knowledge
  - willing to make present
      sacrifices for future gains

People skills need honing
  - not very sensitive to the needs
      of others
  - not very interested in people
  - tends to be abrupt

Overall Summary

Jim Waters has all the makings of a good machinist. He is intelligent, he is strong technically, he qualifies as a hard worker, and he is reasonably mature for his age. Jim did well in high school and particularly well in his apprenticeship training. Because of his conscientiousness and attention to detail, he finds it easy to work to close tolerances. As a result of his summer work with Sperry, Jim has a firsthand understanding of what it is like to work in a factory.

Jim's only shortcomings have to do with lack of leadership potential and people skills. He lacks a number of characteristics of leadership, and is not at all interested in assuming responsibility for the supervision of others. Inclined to be quiet, introverted, and a bit of a loner, Jim prefers to keep to himself. At this stage of his development, he is not all that interested in other people.

In summary, Jim Waters's assets appreciably outweigh his shortcomings for the job of machinist. True, he is not very people-oriented and does not have much leadership potential, but his above-average intelligence, strong technical ability, good motivation, maturity, and academic preparation should enable him to make fine progress in the machine shop. He is rated as definitely "above average."

Overall Rating _____✓_____

Excellent	Above average	Average	Below average	Poor
Best-qualified		*Qualified*	*Not qualified*	

F. J. Brazzy
Signature of interviewer

INTERVIEW RATING FORM

Name   Mary K. Smythe   Date   10/4/82

Interviewed for   Keypunch Operator   Interviewer   Richard Crocker

Summary of Assets

Highly motivated
  - great amount of energy
  - hard worker
  - self-starter

Summary of Liabilities

Not quite as mature as might be desired
  - judgment not always good
  - does not know herself well
  - vocational goals not well-thought-out

(continued)

Excellent mental ability
- highly verbal
- learns very quickly
- perceptive

Good leadership potential
- assertive
- self-confident
- enthusiastic
- communicates well

Good people skills
- tactful
- friendly
- cooperative

Dislike of detail

Becomes rather quickly bored with
routine work

Extroverted

Overall Summary

Mary Smythe has a great deal to commend her. She is bright mentally, has demonstrated the ability to work hard, gets along well with people, and has good leadership potential. Mary has had meaningful summer jobs—jobs which she obtained on her own initiative. She made excellent grades in high school and showed leadership in extracurricular activities.

On the negative side, however, Mary is not as mature as some young people of her age. This is reflected in the fact that she does not know herself very well and has not shown very good judgment in her selection of her first out-of-school job. She has considerable dislike of detail and becomes rather quickly bored with routine work.

In summary, despite her many fine assets and the fact that she has passed all of the preemployment tests, Mary is not appropriately qualified for the job under consideration. Essentially a "people person," she would be completely frustrated in a job with so little contact with others. Probably too bright intellectually for this routine-type work, Mary would become quickly fed up with the excessive detail. For the specific job of keypunch operator, then, Mary's shortcomings outweigh her assets. She is therefore rated "below average." Because of her very fine potential, though, she should be brought back for a second interview, for the purpose of acquainting her with other jobs that might make better use of her abilities.

Overall Rating _____ ✓ _____

Excellent	Above average	Average	Below average	Poor
Best qualified		*Qualified*	*Not qualified*	

Richard Crocker

Signature of interviewer

Interview Guide

I. Work history
    A. Relevance of prior jobs.
        1. Similar job duties
        2. Any experience working shifts or weekends?
        3. Experience with the required hand or machine tools?
        4. Similar working conditions?
            a. Similar environmental factors such as noise, heat, or hazardous conditions?
            b. Used to close supervision?
            c. Any duties detail-oriented?
            d. Any experience with routine work?
    B. Likes.
    C. Dislikes.
    D. Conditioning to work.
    E. Earnings (starting and ending).
    F. Reasons for changing jobs.
        1. Unsound reasons for leaving jobs?
        2. Does applicant typically get another job before leaving the previous one?
    G. Reaction to supervisors and coworkers.
        1. "How did you *feel about* your supervisor?"
        2. "How did you *feel about* the people you worked with?"
    H. Attendance on last job.
        1. "How many days of work did you miss last year?"
    I. Career goals.
        1. "What does a job have to have to give you satisfaction? For some people it's money, for some it's security, for some it's the satisfaction of working with their hands, for some it's the satisfaction of working as a member of a team, for some it's the chance to work on their own without close supervision. What's important to you?" (Variety versus routine; fair amount of pressure or not so much; concentrated work or not so much.)
        2. "Why do you want to work for this company?"
        3. "What do you know about us?"
        4. "What kind of job do you want?"
        5. "What are your salary expectations?" (Realistic?)
        6. "Where do you see yourself 5 years from now?"

II. Education.
   A. Best- and least-liked subjects.
   B. Grades.
      1. "What about grades? Were they average, above average, or perhaps somewhat below average?"
   C. Extracurricular activities.
      1. Sports, public office, music, clubs?
   D. Effort.
      1. "How conscientious a student were you? Did you work about as hard as the average person, a little harder, or not quite as hard?"
   E. Non-high school graduates.
      1. "How did you happen to leave school?"
   F. Training since high school.
      1. On-the-job training.
      2. Evening courses.
      3. Correspondence courses.
   G. Interviewer's mental review of applicant's education.
      1. Relevance.
         a. Sufficient formal education as prescribed in worker specifications?
         b. Subject preferences related to job requirements?
         c. Required mathematical or mechanical aptitude?
         d. Required on-the-job or other special training?
      2. Has the applicant done about as well as might be expected in light of what he or she has to work with?
III. Outside interests and hobbies.
   A. Participate in any community activities?
   B. Any reading? What kind and how much?
   C. Any sports or other physical activities?
IV. Self-evaluation.
   A. Strengths.
      1. "If we were to contact your previous supervisors, what do you think they would say about your strengths? Would they say that you worked harder than the average person, got along better with people, had a better attendance record, were more reliable—what would they say?"
   B. Shortcomings.
      1. "What would they say you could improve? No one is perfect; we all have some things we could improve. Would they say you could use a little more patience, do a better job of getting to work on time, control your temper a little better, be more aggressive—what would they say?"

INDEX